PROMISES OF HOPE

PROMISES OF HOPE

◆

One mother's journey of hope for her son,
and faith in a God of promises.

C. Denise Knox

iUniverse, Inc.
New York Lincoln Shanghai

PROMISES OF HOPE
One mother's journey of hope for her son, and faith in a God of promises.

Copyright © 2007 by C. Denise Knox

All rights reserved. No part of this book may be used or reproduced by any means, graphic, electronic, or mechanical, including photocopying, recording, taping or by any information storage retrieval system without the written permission of the publisher except in the case of brief quotations embodied in critical articles and reviews.

iUniverse books may be ordered through booksellers or by contacting:

iUniverse
2021 Pine Lake Road, Suite 100
Lincoln, NE 68512
www.iuniverse.com
1-800-Authors (1-800-288-4677)

Because of the dynamic nature of the Internet, any Web addresses or links contained in this book may have changed since publication and may no longer be valid.

The views expressed in this work are solely those of the author and do not necessarily reflect the views of the publisher, and the publisher hereby disclaims any responsibility for them.

ISBN: 978-0-595-44716-9 (pbk)
ISBN: 978-0-595-89037-8 (ebk)

Printed in the United States of America

When Matthew was thrown in jail on July 21, 2001, I had mountains of mixed feelings. I knew his life was coming to a boiling point. With drugs, alcohol, stealing and living the wild life he had chosen to live, it couldn't and wouldn't last long. Not with the promise God had given me for his life.

This was a promise I was soon going to question. I would even question the very existence of a loving, kind God whom I had believed in all of my life, and had raised my children to believe in.

Soon, way too soon, my faith would be put to the ultimate test. Do I truly believe? Is He really a God of love and mercy? How could He be so cruel to those He's supposed to love so much?

Today, I know the answer to these questions, without any doubt. This is my journey.

Denise Knox

I want to dedicate this book to my family and friends who have shared this journey with us. Without them, it would have been a very lonely road to walk. I want to thank my sister Stacy and my dear friend Tobi for being there for me, even during their own pain and grief. There were days when I just needed a breathing person at the other end of the phone line and they were there. Sometimes all I would do was cry and they would cry with me. No words, no attempts at trying to make it better; just sharing the pain and loss together. What a blessing from God they have been.

I especially want to thank my cousin-in-law, Kathy. In November of 2003, my father-in-law passed away after a lengthy hospital stay. As the family was gathered together in my mother-in-law's kitchen after the funeral, I had the opportunity to share with them what God was doing in my life to ease my pain, and I shared some of the miracles He had performed. I testified of how the Lord was bringing so much together to make sense now what I couldn't see before. I know the Holy Spirit was there with us and many of them listened intently. I had no idea the full affect of this conversation until about a week later when I received a card from Kathy.

She thanked me for sharing my testimony and told me how she could feel Matthew's presence in her life. She too was struggling with a teenager, but through this testimony, she now felt she could control her fears and renew her faith. She felt God had sent a message through me to Matthew and then back to her. She felt God had her at that place at that moment so she could be reassured of how strong His presence was in our lives.

It was then that the Holy Spirit told me that this testimony was to be shared with every one. That was the defining moment when I realized that Matthew's life was to shine for the glory of God and as a testimony of the goodness of our Creator. At that moment, Matthew Dean had become "a mighty man of valor" for God.

Contents

INTRODUCTION xi
CHAPTER 1   GIFTS OF GOD 1
CHAPTER 2   THE PROPHECY SPOKEN 9
CHAPTER 3   SEARCHING FOR LOVE. 18
CHAPTER 4   PAIN AND SORROW. 26
CHAPTER 5   A MIND UNRENEWED 39
CHAPTER 6   THE WOOD PILE 51
CHAPTER 7   A PROFESSION OF FAITH. 60
CHAPTER 8   THE KNOCK ON THE DOOR. 73
CHAPTER 9   THE MIRACLES BEGIN 92
CHAPTER 10 DID YOU KNOW MATT? 106
CHAPTER 11 ONE SET OF FOOTPRINTS. 115
CHAPTER 12 A CALL TO PARENTS 121
EPILOGUE 129

INTRODUCTION

The pages of this book began in a note pad. I had felt an urgency to jot down these revelation words and all the acts of love that the Lord was raining on me as time began to pass after that tragic day.

I knew I was closer to Him than ever before, even though my heart did not feel Him. But these gifts of love were entirely too important to miss or to forget. I had to keep them close to me.

As I felt the love of God become more and more evident in this situation, I knew that this journey was something that had to be shared. Soon the jotted down notes became a journal and then, by the leading of the Holy Spirit, the journal became this book.

Way too often we get so busy in our lives that we sometimes miss the little things the Lord does for us on a regular basis. It is so sad that sometimes it takes a tragedy for us to fall to our knees and completely surrender our all to the Lord, all that we have and all that we are. It is not necessary to wait until a tragedy occurs. God's abundant love is available to us all. It is ours for the taking at any time.

I never understood just how intimately the Lord loves each of us, individually and equally, until this time in my life. My sincere prayer is that this testimony of the grace and love of our Almighty God, Creator and Father will touch every life that it reaches out to; that you, too, will see just how much your heavenly Father loves you and wants to bestow that love on you.

He is a good God. His love for us knows no boundaries. What He has done for me, He has done and will do for all who trust in Him. And He's only just begun.

1

GIFTS OF GOD

It seemed as though God had touched Matthew's life from the very beginning. Even his delivery, which was less than three and one half-hours long, was very special. It was an easy delivery: quick, with no complications. We had been given the gift of a perfectly healthy, beautiful little boy, born Sunday evening, April 29, 1979.

The whole time during the pregnancy I had settled on the name Andrew Dean. I had always loved the names Andrew and Nicholas. Dean would be after my husband, whose middle name is Dean. I couldn't get much of a response out of my husband on the names; he only gave his opinion if it was a name he insisted on *not* having, one of which was Nicholas. He had said that we were not going to have a son going through life with the name Nick Knox! I agreed and moved on to Andrew. I could tell my husband wasn't completely thrilled with the name, but he made no other suggestions ... at least not until our son's birth.

With such a quick delivery, I tore a little and the doctor had to give me a couple of stitches. It was then that I realized I had had no medication for delivery. I asked the doctor if I had just given birth naturally and he said, "Mrs. Knox, if you'd have done it any more natural, you would have had him in a corn field!"

As I laid back in awe in my husband Dennis's arms, thrilled that this little bundle was finally here, they brought our new baby boy over to us.

The nurse held him up for us to gaze upon and asked us his name. Before I could say anything, Dennis jumped in and proudly said, "Matthew." I quickly turned and looked at Dennis in shock and asked, "Matthew? Where did that name come from?" "I don't know. I just like it." He had almost as much of a shocked look on his face as I'm sure I did. But that was that! Matthew Dean it was.

I later learned that the meaning of the name Matthew is "Gift of God"! Oh how true that was! It would be many years later before I would learn the full extent of that gift of our son on that day. It took quite a long time to also recognize the hand of God in that moment. Where had that name come from? It had come from the Holy Spirit. His name had been designed by God.

From the beginning, He had intervened and named our son.

We were so overwhelmed with love for this little bundle that it just can not be put into words. We were very blessed.

The very next Sunday we took him to church and gave him right back to God. We had him dedicated to the Lord at a little local Assembly of God church in Big Bear, California, where we were living with my mom and step dad at the time. It was a day I've never forgotten. I was so engulfed in emotions that I almost embarrassed myself. The three of us were called up to the platform with the pastor so he could pray for us. It seemed as if God's presence was right there on that platform with us, letting us know He had His hand on us and Matthew was His. The whole congregation prayed for us and the room was charged with His presence. It was a monumental moment for me. I wept almost uncontrollably and my heart was bursting with thankfulness for my family, and especially for this precious little boy.

Twenty-eight months later we were blessed again with a baby girl. There were many complications that came with the pregnancy and her delivery, but God was there with us once more and I knew His grace and love would see us through.

At my first ultra-sound with this pregnancy, they found a growth on my right ovary. By the suspicious way the nurse was acting, I could tell something was wrong. She wouldn't give me my ultra sound picture and told me that the doctor would contact me. When he did, all he said was that there was an abnormal growth on my right ovary. They couldn't tell if it was cancerous or not. We just had to go through the pregnancy watching, waiting and praying. It was a long, torturous wait. Somewhere around seven and a half months they decided the tumor was growing faster than the baby, so it was time to remove the tumor.

We were now living at my sister's in California. We had moved back to Missouri when Matthew was only one month old, but there were no jobs and things were hard. Two years later my family came back to move my grandmother out of her house and out to California, and they offered for us to come too. The three of us were cramped in one small bedroom; Dennis and me with Matthew in his crib. Matthew was two and a half years old now and he was anxiously waiting for his baby sister to get here. At about 6 weeks before my due date we went into the hospital on a Wednesday afternoon and on Thursday morning I had major surgery to remove the tumor.

I am so thankful my sister and brother-in-law are Christians. They and their entire church had been praying for us. Some how I felt everything would be ok, but I was still frightened for my baby's life. They sliced me open and pulled my womb to the side, cut out the tumor along with my ovary, then pushed my womb back into place and stapled me back together. I had twenty-one staples in my stomach. I know this sounds incredible but it is true. My doctor told me I am in a medical book somewhere for unusual surgeries.

Early the next morning I awoke to my water breaking and within an hour and a half, my darling daughter was here. Again, this birth happened so quickly there was no time to prepare for medication. Even with the staples in my stomach, I was able to give birth naturally.

The cord was wrapped around my daughter's neck when she was delivered, and she wasn't breathing. I hadn't noticed the eerie silence in the delivery room when she was first born. I was so thrilled at them telling me I had my baby girl that I hadn't even noticed that my husband had laid his head in my shoulder and was quietly crying. The doctor was taking care of me and it soon hit me that my baby wasn't crying. I began to panic and frantically asked them, "Why isn't she crying? What's wrong, Dennis what's going on?" I tried to come up off of the table to see her and Dennis grabbed me by my shoulders to lay me back down. No words came out of his mouth. He just buried his head back into my shoulder, silently wept and held me. All I knew at the time was I had my little girl, my Sabra Diane.

Her name had come to us through someone we met before she was born. We had met a young couple in Texas and the woman's name was Sabra. We had never heard this name before and as soon as she spoke it I knew that was going to be my little girl's name if I ever had one. God had a plan designed from the beginning of time and three weeks later after meeting that couple, we discovered we were pregnant. Eight months later, we were blessed with this precious gift from God.

The doctor was trying to assure me that every thing would be ok and every one was doing everything they could. I saw several professionals surrounding her and working desperately to help her. It took what seemed like forever for them to get her to breathe. But she eventually let out that most glorious new born cry. She was severely jaundiced and in need of an incubator, but she was a good weight and absolutely beautiful. She stopped breathing again in the nursery with most all of my family watching through the nursery window. The nurses closed the curtains and called in her pediatrician. Her doctor began working on her again and there were quite a few intense moments as the family stood by and waited, but with the hand of God in control of these wonderful doctors and nurses and everyone in prayer for her, Sabra was fine.

The doctor had released me from the hospital but Sabra was not ready to go home yet. I refused to leave the hospital without her. She had to stay in the incubator for a week before she was released to go home and I, by the grace of God, was able to stay in the hospital with her as long as there was a bed available. It was a long week of watching this brand new baby girl get stuck with needles. She had an I.V. in her temple and her little head was shaved on one side and out of proportion from the pressure of the cyst. She was kept under a heat lamp the whole time but occasionally I would get to feed her and hold her. We bonded as best we could in that cold and sterile atmosphere. Once she was released from the hospital, we headed home to Dad and her big brother "Bubby". Matthew was very anxious to see his baby sister. Now having both a boy and girl, we were the perfect family. This was my life and I was more than ready to live it. I had been twice blessed and Sabra was immediately dedicated to God on her first Sunday home. This also was an overwhelming experience. The presence of God was so powerful. My heart was so full of thanks for the miracle of my daughter's birth. No cancer was found and I had a wonderful family that my Father had provided me with.

2

THE PROPHECY SPOKEN

Right from the beginning I had raised my kids in church and taught them as much as I knew about Jesus and God's Word. I knew I was not a perfect person and we were young and made many mistakes. But I was determined to teach my children about God and raise them the way the Lord expected me to. I was going to walk in the light He had given me and, with His help, I was determined to do my best for my family.

One Sunday evening, when Matthew was five years old (just one week shy of his 6th birthday), we had a guest speaker come to our little Assembly of God church in Riverside, CA. The speaker was the leader of a group of young men from Teen Challenge. These young men that accompanied him had formed a choir and they ministered to people through this outreach. That night they were reaching out to the men in the congregation to be men of God and to not play games, but to take their roles as men of God seriously. I don't remember much more about them or the sermon, but I do remember the altar call.

The altar call was given specifically for the men. I was so thankful to see my husband go to the altar, along with almost every man there. All of the women, including myself, sat in the front pews praying for our men and what the Lord was doing in their lives. Matthew was sitting by my side and I noticed he was sobbing. I asked him what was wrong and at first he cried and told me that he didn't know. Then I asked him if he wanted to pray and he cried, "Yes. I want Jesus in my heart."

At that moment we prayed together and he asked Jesus in his heart at the tender age of five. But that wasn't enough for him. The Holy Spirit was moving on Matthew and he wanted to go pray with his Dad. Matthew was still sobbing as I let him go to the altar to join his dad in prayer. I stayed in my seat and was sharing and praying with the ladies. I was so pleased at what had just happened, but I hadn't realized the Lord was still moving on my son's little soul.

The next thing I remember doing was looking around to check on Matthew. He had left his daddy's side and was walking around each one of the men at the altar, laying hands on them and praying for them, still weeping. This was such a precious sight to see; my heart was so moved. But at the same time I was concerned he was disturbing the men as they prayed. I began to snap my fingers at him to call him back so that he wouldn't bother them, but the guest speaker stopped me. His name was Alan and he was truly on fire for God. He had brought these young men in to give their testimonies and to call on the men of the church to be sincere men of God. He had been watching Matthew also and he saw the Lord working in this little man's life. He saw the Lord using Matthew to pray for these men. The Holy Spirit was using Matthew to go before the Lord with the pure heart of a child and lay hands on these men and pray for them.

Alan stepped up to the podium. "Is he your son?" he asked. I said, "Yes," I answered. When he asked me his name, I told him it was Matthew and he began to speak words of wisdom over my little boy. It was a prophecy. He said, "Matthew is going to be a mighty man of valor for God. He will know much pain and sorrow, and God is preparing him with a sensitive heart now, but he will be a mighty man of valor for God."

I sat stunned by what had just happened. My son had just been prophesied over and at that moment I knew the Lord's arms were wrapped around my Matthew and God had a plan for his life. I received it, I believed it and I would spend my life standing on it. Oh the joy that sprung up in my heart! I praised and thanked the Lord for the security of knowing my son's future.

I asked my husband later that evening if he had heard what Alan had said. He said he had not heard what was said but he knew something was going on. I shared with him what had happened at the altar, and to my surprise he became upset. It hurt him to think Matthew would know much pain and sorrow. He didn't understand why God would put that on him. Dennis asked me intensely, "Why did he have to say that? Why does he have to have sorrow?" At the time I didn't have much of an explanation, but I believed God only had good planned for our son and we thanked God for the promise on our son's life. I stood firm from that moment on, that one day this prophecy would be fulfilled in Matthew's life. I wrote it down on a small piece of paper and dated it. I put it in my Bible and it remains there to this day.

The kids and I began to participate in almost everything our church offered. We attended every Wednesday and on Sunday mornings, and most of the Sunday night services too. Matthew and Sabra were involved in Royal Rangers and Missionettes and I was the assistant coordinator of the Missionette program at our church. This is a church group for the kids, similar to Boy Scouts and Girl Scouts. The one major difference is all the classes are revolved around Christ and biblical teachings. During one of the Royal Ranger meetings, when Matthew was about eight years old, one of the leaders was telling the boys about Jesus. He asked them if they had Jesus in their hearts and led the ones that weren't sure to the Lord. Matthew had said he didn't know for sure so again he asked Jesus in his heart and the following Sunday he was baptized. His heart was so tender towards the Lord and we were so proud of him. The foundation had been set; he knew who Jesus was personally. Matthew had taken the step of baptism and with the prophecy spoken over his life, I knew he would continue to walk with God. The Lord had great plans for Matthew.

As he grew into a teen, things began to change dramatically. One of his closest friends died in the 1993 flood that swept through the Midwest and devastated many in the country as well as here in Missouri. This was the first death and funeral in Matthew's life and it deeply affected him. He was only fourteen at the time and he immediately began to close up his deepest thoughts and feelings.

Losing his best friend had dramatically changed Matthew, and he began to struggle with his Christian walk. Even though we were a close family and felt that open communication was very important, he continued to become more rebellious. Matthew was well aware that he could talk with us at any time about anything—and sometimes he did, whether it was with me, his father, or his sister. But his attitude continued to get worse and worse. Whether it was due to his hurt and anger over the loss of his best friend, the mistakes we had made as parents, the fact that he was just being a teenager, or all three, I can not say. But it didn't take long for the hurt and anger to grasp hold of his life and he soon turned to a life of rebellion and drugs.

As the drugs and disrespect began to get out of hand, I knew it was time to take drastic measures. I had to get him out of the house. He was now seventeen, almost eighteen, and like most seventeen year olds, he thought he knew more than his parents did. He was convinced that the outside world was so much better than home. One day his anger got out of control as we argued and he drew his fist back as if to hit me. That was it. I escorted him out the front door and threw some clothes out after him. It was my first step of "tough love" and one of the hardest things I had ever done, up to that point. When situations like this would arise with Matthew, I would go to my Bible and take out that little piece of paper with the prophecy on it and I would hold it up to God and remind Him of His promise over my son. I would read it to Him and pray for this promise to hurry up and come to pass. Then I would read the part of the prophecy that said he would know much pain and sorrow and I would humble myself before the Lord and cry. I would surrender the situation to my Father and ask Him to just keep my Matthew safe and to give me His strength and wisdom to see this through.

Throwing Matthew out of the house and sending him to live on his own started a pattern for him. This was Matthew's first of several encounters with older girls with children. These young mothers would take care of him. He loved kids. Even when he was a ten year old little boy, if you would have asked him what he wanted to be when he grew up, he would have told you, "a daddy", so this seemed the easy way out for him. He met a young girl with a two-year-old daughter and she had her own apartment. He was set. He felt he didn't need us or any of our rules anymore. He could make up his own. He thought he was on top of the world and he had it made. He had no job, he had quit school, and he had no money coming in to help pay the bills and no money to or help pay for food. Needless to say he and this girl didn't last long. I don't think Matthew really meant to, but she soon saw he was just using her to be out of the house. He saw it as being on his own and was enjoying the freedom of being independent. But, of course, he actually wasn't on his own. He was now dependent on her and she was now raising another child. They started fighting a lot and he became angry that she expected anything from him. It was like being back at home for him. He had someone constantly expecting him to be responsible, to work, and carry his share of the load. He didn't like that at all so their relationship didn't last too long.

My prayers for him never ceased. I was concerned for him constantly and prayed for God to keep him safe and bring him to his senses and his knees. He had been raised to live a better life and he knew better. His dad is a hard working man. He was never without a job purposely, and we always had what we needed. That's not to say we didn't hit hard times, there were many. But we never went without food or shelter and all the necessities. This was not only due to hard work, but I know the Lord's hand was upon our lives.

Matthew knew the life of hard work and faith in God and that they both pay off. God is faithful, but we must do our part. I just couldn't understand who this young man was any more. He was becoming a stranger to me. He was living a life of little values and morals, but when he got into trouble it was always Mom and Dad he came to; he knew I was constantly praying for him. I was always reminding him of the prophecy over his life and telling him he needed to yield to this because God had a plan for his life and the life he was living was not it.

A couple of times I tried to pray the prayer of, "Whatever it takes Lord, have your way with Matthew," but I was always holding something back. I didn't have enough faith to pray that prayer and trust in God to do what was best for Matthew. I tried to always stand on God's Word and the prophecy that was spoken over Matthew. I believed with all my heart that he would some day return to the Lord and sell out completely to Jesus. I was convinced that all the things he was to go through now were going to be used as a great testimony in his ministry that was to come later on in his life. I stood on this promise for 17 years.

Matthew moved in and out of our house quite a bit during this time. Sometimes he would stay with friends and occasionally he would even get a job that would last for a few paychecks. Then one day he would decide not to show up and he would lose the job. He always had an excuse for missing a day of work. When he would get fired, according to him, it was always someone else's fault. Then there would be talk of him and a friend getting a place together but nothing would ever develop. I could see him slipping further away from his roots of Christ and from us. All I could do was pray.

3

SEARCHING FOR LOVE

One day Matthew came home and told me of this new girl he had just met. His eyes were lit up and he seemed to have that old spark back in his life. She was almost five years older than he was and she had two little girls. He immediately decided he was in love with her and they were going to get a place together. He wanted me to meet her and I told him of my concerns of him living with another girl. He had been taught that this was not an appropriate way to live, but at the same time I was so happy to see him happy. Not only was he in love with *her*, but he had fallen in love with those two little girls also. One was four years old and the other one was about eleven months. I must admit they were adorable and I fell in love with them too—all three of them.

They quickly found a place together and he started working. It seemed like he was doing much better and was settling down. Being in love and having this family seemed to build his self-respect, confidence, and positive motivation. They were very happy for awhile, but without Christ in our relationships, we leave an open door for the enemy to come in and destroy it all. Along with not being married, they dabbled with drugs, drank, and partied a lot, so I knew this happiness wouldn't last long. Even so, I had hoped it would work out. Matthew had started out so much more responsible with her than he had with the other women, and he dearly loved those two precious girls. The younger one had even begun to call him "Daddy". We talked about the dangers of that, but it made him feel so proud to be a "dad". Since this girl couldn't have any more children, he was claiming these two as his. They meant the world to him and as far as he was concerned, his future was set.

I took the girls to church every chance I got and always witnessed to Matthew and the girls' mother. She and Matthew even went to church a time or two with me, but there was no significant change in their lifestyles. As far as I knew, she had never made a complete surrender to Christ with all her heart and Matthew was harboring anger, pain and rebellion. Unfortunately, they enjoyed the lives they led and they weren't ready to give them up.

They were together for over three years and somewhere around the middle of the second year, I think the newness had begun to wear off. Matthew began to work less and I could see the evidence of drugs becoming more and more apparent in his life. Of course with the drugs and the drinking and the lack of work, they began to fight more and his life was full of turmoil. Drinking became almost a constant thing with him, and I could see a pattern of addiction falling into place. He wasn't having fun if drugs and alcohol weren't involved.

I was not walking the walk at this time in our lives either. I talked the talk, I would profess Christ and my belief in God at any time in any place, but I would also confess I wasn't where He wanted me to be in my life. I knew in my heart I would one day soon get back on track, but without a family church and regular attendance, without daily doses of the Word, and without spiritual leadership, life is sure to take a wrong turn. I allowed this to happen in my life. The church we had attended for so long when the kids were little had had a big upset. The married pastor ran off with the married song leader, and they were not married to each other. The church split up. The faithful members stayed and saw it through, but I let this discourage me and I quit going to that church; then it started to become much easier to walk *with* the world than to fight *against* it. It was much easier to go with the flow of the world than to fight against the current and be separate unto God. I was growing weary of the fight against drugs and alcohol that were so prevalent in our family.

This was a time when I had slipped into an attitude of not wanting to feel so separated from my husband and the people that were now in our lives. I let the cares of the world weigh me down instead of keeping my eyes on Christ. This was a very unsatisfying time in all of our lives. I had left my place of spiritual authority over my family and left an open door for the enemy to come in and try to destroy us all. He tried many time to destroy us, but praise God it didn't last long.

Soon my spirit became hungry for worship and fellowship with my Lord, and I would try to find a new church. I would visit many of the local churches, but none of them seemed to fill my needs. They were not what I was looking for. I hungered for a church full of the presence of God, and a powerful congregation and pastor where I could be spiritually fed and start growing again in the Lord. Most of the churches I visited didn't offer that. They were dry and uneventful. I needed the moving of the Holy Spirit. That seemed foreign to a lot of these churches and that was very sad to me, so I would give up again looking for that "perfect church," but only for awhile. The Lord wasn't letting go of me.

The kids had grown up and they didn't want to go to church with me anymore. Of course, Matthew had moved out and was on his own and Sabra was now in high school. She would go with me occasionally and my husband had quit going pretty much altogether. He would go sometimes on the holidays, but that was about it. It became so easy to just stay home than to keep searching and always feeling so disappointed.

I was not as disappointed with church and the people as I was in waiting on God. I knew people would fail me, even church people. Christians are human and walking in the same world as I am. I didn't put my faith in people, but I did expect more from my Father. I was getting pretty tired of waiting for that prophecy to be fulfilled in Matthew's life and I needed God to get with it.

I did attend a church about twenty five miles away one day called Church on The Rock. I was overwhelmed by the presence of God in this place. This one kept calling me back. When I did get up and go to church, that's where I would attend. I could feel the presence of the Lord all over that place even before I got through the front doors. I would be so overcome with His presence in the services and I would try to set things right with God, but I was holding something back. I would attend for a few weeks, then I would get lazy again. I would tell the Lord I needed something smaller, somewhere closer and more personal. I again would try a different church but would always leave disappointed and feeling empty, then my spirit would cry out for a touch from God and I would go back to Church on The Rock. I never left there feeling empty or disappointed. The Lord let me know this was the place He had for me, but I hadn't taken that step to turn my life back around yet. I had gotten out of step with God's plan for my life, but I hadn't lost sight of what I needed to do.

At the time I kept making excuses for myself not to become a member. I told the Lord I wouldn't join a church until my husband joined with me, or it was too far to drive and it was too large. Life just wasn't turning out the way I had planned and hoped it would be. I began to get frustrated with God because He wasn't making everyone change the way I wanted Him to. I completely missed out on the fact that *I* needed to change. Wow! I guess I had forgotten that we are free-will beings. God created us that way and He will not force anyone to change if they do not want to. No matter how hard I prayed for my family, they had to make that decision for themselves, and so did I. I had to decide to let go of them and let God do a work in me before He could do a work in them. Eventually, after several guilt-ridden and empty years had gone by, I quit rebelling and surrendered my life back to the Lord. I still hadn't made the commitment to a church home yet, but I knew God had a place for me and He and I were working things out.

Without any real change in his life, Matthew had begun to get into quite a bit of trouble. He was getting into trouble with the police, he owed people money for drugs and he was constantly avoiding someone. Then we started getting collect calls from Matthew from jail. Usually it was something minor or just plain dumb. He was acting without thinking. He was driving drunk, he didn't pay a fine, he was driving without plates on the car or he was just driving crazy and reckless. Whatever the case may have been, the calls started to become more frequent and more costly. He had his driver's license suspended after so many run-ins with the police and now he was facing court dates and fines. The more things went wrong with him and his girlfriend, the more trouble with the law he got into.

When they finally broke up, it seemed to be nasty. He didn't talk much about it but I could tell he was truly hurt. He just stayed drunk and high and they would do every thing they could to hurt each other. They tried to work things out and got back together a couple of times, but it was too late. One of the worst parts of this break up was losing those two little girls from our lives. They were quite a bit older now, and they loved Matthew very much and they were very hurt by his leaving. He cut them out completely. He felt it was best just to go forward and not look back, so he came back home, but only temporarily.

4

PAIN AND SORROW

Matthew had a court date I had to take him to one morning and he ran into an old acquaintance, a girl he had known slightly when he was in Jr. High. I had known her parents and their lifestyles and I was not happy to see him catching her eye. This was big trouble for Matthew and I knew it in my spirit.

I should have kept my mouth shut because he decided right then and there that he was going to go home with her when they got out of court. I tried my best to talk him out of it. He had just gotten out of one bad relationship; it was time to cool down and get his head on straight. But he wouldn't hear of it. He left the courtroom with her that afternoon, seemingly pleased with his accomplishments. They came by the house later that evening and I was very surprised he brought her over. He wanted me to see she wasn't like her family and he tried his best to get my approval. He left with her again that night and the next thing I knew they were planning on getting a place together.

I had a really bad feeling about this one. I knew her family and as weak as Matthew was when it came to influence, I didn't see him doing good at all with her. We were nice to her and tried to accept her. I really did not have much of a choice. It was accept her or lose Matthew, and I wasn't about to lose him.

It was during this time I had recommitted my life to Christ. I got so sick of my separation from God I knew I had to do something. I had such a hunger in my heart to do the right thing and to be the intercessor that my family needed. The day I surrendered my all to Him, I sold out to God completely, and I meant every word. The day had finally arrived where I would no longer put my husband, kids, or anything else before my relationship with God. Those days of walking in the flesh were now over and I was moving forward, with or without them. I was back on track with a vengeance. The Lord had put a great hunger in my heart for Him and His word. I knew I had to get back on track with the Lord and be the prayer warrior my family needed. The Lord flooded my spirit with faith, hope, and wisdom; I knew I was growing quickly to a new level in Him.

I was now seeing my Matthew spiral quickly down deeper into the world of drugs and sin. His drug addiction was getting so much worse. The turmoil in his life and the people he associated with were heart breaking. I knew this girl was bad for him and the whole relationship seemed to be based on him not having to live at home and the availability of drugs through their friends and her family.

They had only been together a few weeks when the two of them came to me and Matthew told me he was going to be a father. I knew instinctively that it was not his baby. I tried to tell him this but he argued with me and stood firm that this was his baby. This was all he ever really wanted out of life. I knew in my heart if this had been his baby, he would have made a great turn around in his life for his child. He would have done whatever it took to be a good father, and he would have been a great dad. I also knew in my heart that this baby was not his. But he was convinced that he was finally going to be a dad and that was all he cared about. All we could do as his parents was to wait and see and pray.

We tried to be a family to her and her little boy. She had never had much of a family life and I prayed that maybe God would be able to use us to be good influences for her. I tried to show her a better way of living through Christ and I even led her to the Lord one day. But this whole relationship was all wrong. Now, at this point in time, they were only together because of the baby.

My family got together and gave her a baby shower. This was something that her own family had not cared enough to do for her. I prayed with all my heart that I was wrong about this child and that it was Matthew's, but only for Matthew's sake. I did not want to see him hurt anymore and I knew what this was going to do to him when he found out that this baby wasn't really his. She was going to crush him in the end. I just didn't want to see him go through more disappointment, more pain and more sorrow. But after all, I kept telling myself that this was all a part of his prophecy. He had to know pain and sorrow to be the man of valor that God had promised me he was called to be.

When the baby did arrive, it was a little girl. They named her after me and even gave her Matthew's last name. It was all very sweet, but I just did not feel the attachment to her that a grandmother should. When I looked at her I knew. Matthew was elated with this little bundle and he was waiting for my approval. I just could not give it to him. She was not his and I knew it. I do believe that deep down in his heart he knew this also. He just did not want to face it or admit that he had been wrong. It seemed as though he just wanted someone in his life that belonged to him, someone he could call his own.

We had all been discussing a blood test and she had agreed. I truly believe this girl had convinced herself that this baby was Matthew's. I'm not completely sure as to why, other than she did not want to accept who the real father was, or just that Matthew would be a great dad. The baby had arrived a month early, according to the mother, but not according to the doctors. According to them she was a healthy full term baby girl. So naturally the time frame did not add up. I could see it in Matthew's eyes as it all started to slowly sink in. Soon after the baby was born the three of us went together to get the blood test done. They had both agreed they wanted me there and when we met at the doctor's office that day I saw a dark cloud form over Matthew. My heart was wrenched with pain at what he was going through. My only hope for him was to stand before God, night and day, and claim His promises over Matthew.

We waited for what seemed like forever for the test results to come in. All along this girl was adamant that this was Matthew's child. She said she had not been with any one else for months before they got together and she never wavered. But unfortunately, blood tests don't lie and the test came back negative. This precious little baby girl was not his and he was devastated.

His letter came to our house since he still used our address. Hers had gone to their house, so I knew when he knew. I called him right away to check on him. He said he was fine, but something strange was in his voice. I begged him to come home. I promised him we would be there for him and see him through this, but he refused. I think he just couldn't handle the humiliation of it all. He began to lose complete control. He just didn't care about anything anymore. His drugs and drinking became rampant. He no longer hesitated to come see us stoned and totally wasted.

One day I finally told him not to come to our home any more in that condition. It was so hard to do, but I just couldn't stand to see him like that. He was breaking our hearts and we just didn't know how to help him. I had considered the idea of turning him in to some sort of rehab, but I couldn't bring myself to do it. I was completely convinced God would intervene in this situation. He was hitting his rock bottom and I could not see anywhere else for him to go but to God.

We couldn't understand why he continued to stay with this girl. I believe in my heart, from certain things he said, he just couldn't desert her. She had no one else who really cared about her and so he stayed, but the pain was too great for him. Every day he was helping care for two more children that were not his. He had helped raise the other two from his first relationship for so many years and he had lost them, now this was happening to him. He buried his pain and anger even deeper with more drugs and more alcohol.

Then came another one of those phone calls: collect call from an inmate in St. Charles County jail. He had been arrested again. This time I could tell it was bad. The last few times I had seen him he was strung out and had lost so much weight. He had now gotten to the point were he was taking any kind of drug he was offered. He had even started making some of the stuff. It was a nightmare. He was only twenty-one years old but it seemed he had already lived a lifetime. He was an extremely handsome young man, but the wear and tear of the world were on his face and he was aging quickly.

You could hear the fear and regret in his voice when he called. He began to tell us what had happened. He was caught with a friend stealing junk food from a grocery store late that night. They had been drinking and Matthew was driving without a license. When the store clerks approached them outside of the store, an argument began and the boys jumped in the car and took off. The store clerk called the police and the chase was on. It took several blocks and even a road block before the boys got caught.

When the police finally got them pulled over, they searched the car. They found several boxes of sinus pills in the trunk of the car. These pills were used to make Methamphedemine. They had been going from store to store most of the night stealing these pills before they had decided to steal something to eat.

You really can not put into words the feelings that come over you at a time like this. We were so broken-hearted and disappointed, yet at the same time my heart overflowed with love and tenderness for him. I was also very angry with him because these were just ridiculously stupid actions. These actions were not my son, *not* the boy I had raised in church and watched crying at the altar and being prophesied over. It is so hard to grasp hold of what in a person's life can make them change so dramatically, but it had really taken time. This all had been coming together in Matthew's life for years—hurt after hurt, disappointment after disappointment, and dependence on the world and the pleasures it offered instead of dependence on God.

We get to this level when we continue to constantly reject Christ. As we little by little shut God out, the enemy, Satan, moves right on in. As we close the door on Jesus, we open it to the world and all its evil elements. This happens by the choices we make in our lives. "I think I'll skip church today and sleep in." "I think I'll go to that party and have a couple of drinks." "One hit off that joint isn't going to hurt me." "These people are OK, they have good hearts."

And more than likely these people do have good hearts. Their hearts just do not belong to God and they are blinded by sin. In Psalms 146:8, we are told that "the Lord opens the eyes of the blind: the Lord raises them that are bowed down: the Lord loves the righteous." But as we choose the things of the world over the things of God, the Light of the Lord begins to dim in our lives. Our hearts begin to harden to the voice of God and it gets easier and easier to keep making these bad choices. This is what happens to us when we put the world first and not the Kingdom of God. I had gone through a time in my life where I had put my family first and slid from the will of God. As I allowed this to happen in my life, my lack of prayers over my family had diminished and sin had gotten a foothold on our lives. What a perfect example of Romans 6:16, "Don't you know that when you offer yourselves to someone to obey him as slaves, you are slaves to the one who you obey; whether you are slaves to sin, which leads to death, or to obedience which leads to righteousness?"(NIV) I had willfully chosen to be a slave to disobedience and sin.

"But thanks be to God, that though you used to be slaves to sin, you wholeheartedly obeyed the form of teaching to which you were entrusted. You have been set free from sin and become slaves to righteousness." Romans 6:17 & 18 declare exactly what I did to change my life. So now that God was first in my life again I had a spiritual battle in front of me. I was at war with the enemy and fighting for my family. I knew the devil was trying to destroy what God was building. But I had hope in a promise from God in that prophecy.

We went to his arraignment the next day. As he walked through one of the doors into the courtroom, I barely recognized my son. He had always been such a handsome fellow. When he and his sister were little, they almost looked like twins. They had that white blonde hair and blue green eyes. They looked like little angels. As he grew older his hair became darker, but he always had that handsome face fit for a magazine cover.

As he began to abuse the drugs, he underwent another physical change. Here he was chained to four other brutal looking men. His hair was mussed, his eyes wild, and you could tell he was trying to hide his fear with a cocky, tough guy type of walk. He had lost so much weight and his features were beginning to look hardened. We were devastated at his appearance and it broke our hearts to see him this way. I wanted to jump up and hold my son and shake the daylights out of him at the same time. Matthew was so glad to see us. He tried to talk to us as he walked by but it wasn't allowed. All we could do was sit there in silence and listen to the horrible charges that were being filed against him. He looked terrified as they led him and the four other men back out of the room after they had read the horrible charges. There was attempt to manufacture and distribute methamphetamine, fleeing from an officer, driving while intoxicated, driving on a suspended license and even an attempt to kill a police officer. I thought I would pass out. In my heart I just couldn't understand how he had gone down so far. How much more could happen and how much longer would it take before I would see Matthew's life make that turn around that I had been praying for all these years? How much worse could his life get?

After they led him back out to the jail, we talked with the judge. He told us our son was in big trouble. He was looking at being charged with 15 to 20 years for attempt to manufacture; the attempt to kill a police officer carried its own sentencing. We knew that this charge was just ridiculous. We found out later that when he had fled the scene and he had tried to out run the police, that they had a roadblock set up for them and he swerved to avoid it. He ran an officer off the road in the process and that was his "attempt" charge. He had really made the officers angry and they were out to get him at all costs.

We made sure we were at all his court hearings and we never missed a visit. We decided we weren't going to help financially, though. He got himself into jail so he needed to get himself out. But we didn't desert him.

Yes, we were there for him, but he had to make his own choices and decisions and try to come up with all the money and answers he could to get himself straightened out.

I was praying and believing he would lean on Jesus.

Every time he called and every visit we had was geared around Jesus, forgiveness and prayer. I reminded him constantly of the prophecy over him and that he needed to look to the Lord. God may not get him out of it, but He would surely see him through whatever he had to face. We get ourselves into messes and expect God to miraculously get us out, but most of the time, the Lord doesn't work that way. There are consequences to our actions when we step out of the will of the Father. He *does* take those mistakes and bad choices and turns them into "all things that work together for our good" (Romans 8:28), when we let Him. When we ask Him for forgiveness and step back into walking with Him, He takes our mistakes and turns them into blessings. It is our choice. My prayer was that Matthew would see this.

One morning in my travailing for my son to my Heavenly Father, I finally did it. I prayed the prayer for God to do whatever it took to save my son. To bring him into a knowledge and relationship with Him he never knew was possible. I felt it. I knew I meant it. I myself had come into a place with the Lord where I had the faith to trust God's decisions with my loved ones. I felt a peace in that prayer and I felt His presence.

5

A MIND UNRENEWED

One night, late, Matthew called from jail. He had been in for almost two months now and I could tell by his voice something had happened. I panicked as he cried out "MOM!"

"What's wrong, Matthew, what's happened? Are you alright?"

"Yeah Mom, I had to tell you! I met Jesus tonight!! I was trying to read my Bible and do like you said, but it was like trying to read Chinese. I just couldn't understand any of it. So I got mad. I threw my Bible down on the bed and just prayed, 'God, I do not understand any of this. I do not understand your Word. It is like trying to read Chinese for me and all I know is, I want what my mom's got. And I don't want it to be just because I'm in trouble and in here, I want it to be real!'" Then he cried out, "MOM, I met Jesus tonight! He came into my cell, and now I know what you mean! I met Him tonight and I had to call you and tell you!"

Needless to say I was speechless, but only for a moment. I began to praise God with him over the phone and we talked quite awhile, with tears flowing, about him keeping this moment in his heart. I too, agreed with him that this moment must last from now on, not to let go of this when he got out of jail. We prayed and agreed that this was much more than just the "jail house religion" we hear about. I know he was truly sincere. What more could a mother have asked for!!

What a wonderful God we serve! My son cried out to his Lord and He heard him. In his deepest hour of need, the God of his childhood came to his cell and answered his prayer. I just prayed this was real in his heart and he would hang onto it. That was the most wonderful collect call I had ever had!

He spent a little over three months in county jail, and we finally helped him to get out. His first lawyer was a lazy, crooked attorney who wasn't doing anything but sending him "up the river," trying to make deals over the phone with the prosecutor, and not even wanting to go to court. So we finally stepped in. We found a VERY good and very expensive attorney, but he was worth every penny. He got Matthew out on bail and my son moved back home. He was doing great. I had my boy back. He was living steadily at home for the first time in almost five years.

This had been the deal: if we got him out, he had to come back home and stay with us, not back to her. He would be home so we could make sure he got to all his court dates and meetings, since he didn't have a drivers license or a car, and he had to stay clean—no drugs and no alcohol. He agreed.

It was so wonderful having him back. His eyes were clear, his great sense of humor was back, and that sweet shy smile that meant mischief had just entered the room was back on his face. He was putting on weight and looking healthy again. The color was back in his cheeks and so was the bounce in his steps. He loved to tease and he would tickle your ribs till it felt like they were going to break. He loved to laugh. He was a family man. There was no doubt about it. He loved his family with all his heart and he never was ashamed to show it. It was wonderful having my son back and we had a new best friend. Matthew was growing up. The Lord had restored our son back to us and it was wonderful. We were savoring every moment with him.

Slowly, very slowly, he and this girl began to drift apart. He soon began to realize he had no obligation to her and he began to let her go. They remained friends and he still cared about her kids, no matter who they belonged to. But he was facing the facts and finally beginning the healing process.

Matthew and his sister had grown apart over the years. Sabra hated the drugs he took and the bad choices he made, and she would try to talk to him about it. Most of the time, they would end up arguing and then move on to their separate lives. Eventually, as she grew up and moved out of the house, their different lifestyles ended up driving them apart. After Matthew came back home, however, he began to work on their relationship too. He didn't like her boyfriend very much, but no one would ever be good enough for his little sister (that's just the way it was). Their relationship was beginning to mend back together, bit by bit. They may not have agreed on much in life, but there was never any denying Matthew's deep and devoted love for every member of his family.

During this time I had come into that relationship with my Heavenly Father where I could say, with confidence, I felt His presence closer than I have ever before and I was so sure of the future. The Lord had led me into a Bible college and I had begun working on a degree in Biblical Studies. I was learning to hear the voice of my Lord clearer and clearer, was working harder on listening to the Holy Spirit when He spoke, and doing my best to obey. I was walking hand in hand with my Lord, and I felt His anointing on my life. I was growing in the Lord, absorbing His Word and trusting in Him completely. I had finally sold out completely to my Jesus!

Just before I became a member of Church on the Rock, one of my friends had started a new church. We called it Crossroads of Life church and we started with a building a friend owned. That didn't work out too well so we moved it to our homes. Most of the time, we were at the pastor's house or at our home.

When we met at our house, it was usually in our garage because it had more room than our living room. It was wonderful. I could see my family coming back together and my prayers being answered. God was restoring the relationships and lives that Satan had tried to take.

One weekend before Christmas of 2002, we had a birthday party for Jesus in our garage. I had invited several people, friends and family, and most of them showed up. The pastor's boys were in a band and they offered to play that night, so we had live music, lots of food, fellowship, prayer, and a short message about Christ's birth and the choosing of shepherds to tell of His birth. Then we sang Happy Birthday to Jesus. Matthew and his buddy came. Our closest friends were there with us, along with our daughter and her boyfriend. It was a good evening and I was so happy. God had been doing many wonderful things and I could feel His presence enveloped around me.

Those of us that were there who knew the Lord as our savior were all really concentrating on Matthew's best friend, Gene. His brother had died a violent, unexpected death in July and it really knocked him for a loop. He held lots of anger, blame, resentment, and maybe even some guilt in his heart. It had all led to lots of fighting and drinking from the anger he held onto in his life. Matthew had taken it upon himself to guard Gene and be his new brother, but Matthew wasn't grounding himself in the Word or digging deeper into God's plan for his life. He had kept some of the old friends and was picking up his old ways again.

I had noticed him flirting with drugs again. It was evident the night of Jesus's birthday party, but we didn't speak of it. I prayed and trusted in the Lord to give me guidance and help me to let *Him* do the work in Matthew's life.

All of us felt the presence of the Lord that night. I knew He was working things out in each soul that was there. The Holy Spirit was present and touching lives. I could feel God's presence so close during those days and I knew His Holy Spirit was cloaked around me. I thought it was because I had sold out to Him, finally, and I was pressing in. I was seeking the Kingdom of God first and my heart was full of love for the Lord. I know now that was part of it, but I also can see how He was preparing me for the days ahead, those days ahead where I would insist that God had deserted me, betrayed me, dumped on me and had stopped loving me at all. Only the Lord knew what was coming, and only now can I see just how much He really does love us. He was preparing me spiritually and giving me strength ahead of time for what was to come. The Lord was giving me something to cling to in those worst of my worst days—His presence and a grounding in His word.

Matthew was proudly working at Willerding Welding then, but the lawyer's bills were overwhelming for him. We had refinanced our house and paid for everything. The bill had come to an almost whopping fifteen thousand dollars. Matthew was determined to pay it off, and every week he would give me money out of his check. We had a notebook with a running total in it. In his eyes the balance was not going down fast enough, and he hated the guilt he felt for owing us so much money. This brought about his excuse to make money by doing what he knew best. He would secretly make drugs to sell and pay us off with the money. This is where the spiritual fight had begun. I didn't know the full extent of his involvement with the drugs, but I did know he was on them again and instead of going to my Lord with this situation and leaving it with Him, I began to nag. *"Do not come home high. You have got to get off the booze. You need to go to church and get your life together."* He was now spending more time *out* of the house than *in* the house. He was spending more time with his friends and the partying was beginning again.

As a mother I was desperate. I knew I was fighting the powers and principalities of darkness for my son's life, but little did I know the extent of it. My children had always been my life. My mission in life was to raise them for God. My responsibility in life was to be there for them, to pray for them, to teach them, to support them, and most of all to love them. I tried to be all I could be for them. They were everything to me.

Unfortunately, Matthew had become such a handful early in life that almost all of our energy was focused on him. My daughter was close to perfect in our eyes. She was an honor roll student, quiet, thoughtful, was active in school, and almost never a problem. So, I admit now, she was in some ways neglected. That did not mean we loved her less, we just focused on her less. We put a lot on her shoulders, expecting her to keep doing well and not be a problem. We had one child like that already. Thanks to God and His grace and mercy, she managed to keep her life out of conflict and corruption. Only by the Grace of God has she come through and continued to be strong, grounded and well focused in her life. I thank my Father for her every day. She is our treasure here on earth.

But now that they were adults with their own lives, I had a new focus. It was completely on Jesus. I had finally put my children, my husband and all the past in God's hands and I was looking to a wonderful future with God in control. I had His promises to stand on and I knew that He heard my prayers. My hope was renewed in a future for all of us.

A couple of weeks after Jesus' birthday party, God had been doing something dramatic in Matthew's life. He was meeting up with old acquaintances and making amends by either paying back owed money or re-establishing friendships and putting old grudges behind him. It was amazing. I'm not even sure to what extent all this went to. I only know of those instances he had told me about. Plus, he was starting to think and talk more about the Lord. He and Gene had had many discussions of getting their lives together. They had even discussed getting involved with our little home church we were having and helping in our youth group, once we got one started and Matthew was done with all his legal troubles. The Holy Spirit was definitely working on him.

So many things were coming together at once to make for some kind of Godly perfect timing. First, Grandpa Rod, my step-dad, was coming in from California. He only makes it in once every couple of years, but this was two years in a row. I picked him up from the airport on Tuesday and my dad went with me. We all had lunch together and dropped Rod off at Willerding to be with my sister and his daughter, Stacy. Matthew and his Aunt Stacy worked together there for awhile; in fact, he got her the job there. Most of the time they loved working together, but they fought like brother and sister.

My little sister, twelve years my junior, had always been like my first child and when Matthew came along, she was crazy about him. When he was born, she wasn't allowed in the room, but we were on the first floor, so she managed to make it to a window and admire him from outside. You could see it in her face, a future "partner in crime" so to speak. Then when Sabra was born, she became a little mother to them both. They were hers forever.

Matthew had already quit Willerding by this time and was getting back to his old tricks. He had no job, he was staying out all night again, and there were the signs of the drug use. There was such a conflict going on. We were on him about finding a job and keeping his act together. I could see him slipping back into his old life, yet at the same time, I saw the pull of the Holy Spirit on him. He was so close to the end of this legal mess that had been hanging over his shoulders for over a year, and now he was messing up again, sliding backwards instead of moving forward.

We were all supposed to meet in Winfield for dinner the night Rod got in—my dad, Rod, Stacy, her husband and kids, Matthew, Sabra and her boyfriend, and Dennis and me. It was to be a family dinner to celebrate Rod's visit. Nothing worked out right. Stacy's crew had gone to the wrong restaurant, Sabra, her boyfriend and my dad all went to the right restaurant and no one ever showed up. Dennis and I had gotten into an argument on the way there and we turned around and went back home. Satan was really fighting to destroy us all. He was trying to destroy all of these newly established relationships and all the things that God had been rebuilding in us. You could feel the turmoil in the air. It is so amazing to see how blessed we all are to have been able to stay on good terms when all this was happening. That night evil was trying to tear us apart, get us at each other's throats and cause strife. But the mercy of the Lord endures forever. "O give thanks unto the Lord for He is good, for

His mercy and loving-kindness endures forever (Psalms 107:1)."

He kept us together. Everyone stayed calm and we worked everything all out. I know it was the presence of the Holy Spirit. He knew how important these days were and what kind or harsh words would mean in the near future. What a good, merciful and loving God we serve. He is good.

6

THE WOOD PILE

That next morning, Wednesday, I was getting wood for our wood stove and stacking it up on the porch. We had two wood piles: one was of split wood and the other pile was of big logs that still needed to be split. I was getting the split wood. I had no reason to mess with the big logs. My guys still needed to split those, but the Holy Spirit tugged at my heart to go to the big log pile. I was trying to ignore this urge because it just did not make any sense to me to do this. At first I did not realize that a supernatural experience was unfolding. With every load of wood I put in the wheel barrel, I kept feeling the Lord urge me to go to the log pile. It was astonishing how we almost argued out loud! I did not even recognize these thoughts at first as the voice of the Holy Spirit. Just each time I walked up to the wood, I felt a strong urgency to reach for a big log. As I would walk back down to the house, I was talking to myself about it and even talking to the Lord as to why in the world I was feeling like this. Finally, after about five trips with the wheel barrel up and down the hill to get wood, I gave in and walked up to the big log pile. I stood there for a moment wondering what to do and why was I even there. Then I felt the Lord tell me to move the wood and I began to look through the logs. There to my surprise was a trash bag, buried deep down in the woodpile. I still didn't have a clue what this was or what was happening. I asked myself, or actually I asked the Lord, what this was, but without waiting for an answer, I just left it there.

I truly wish I could have seen this through spiritual eyes. I know Satan was trying to blind me from the truth, and the Holy Spirit was trying to lead me into it. I was in the midst of a great spiritual battle. I had actually put the wood back and I was headed back to the house when the Lord spoke to me. "LOOK IN THE BAG!" Those words I could not ignore. As I returned to the big log pile, I was more in awe at the presence of the Lord than anything else. I smiled and laughed to myself at His awesomeness and my hard-headedness. At this point I was more impressed by Him talking to me so audibly than I was at what He was actually saying, that is until I pulled out the trash bag and I opened it.

Inside this kitchen trash bag was my small black overnight bag. I still did not have a clue as to what was happening. I just stood there for a few moments, looking into this kitchen trash bag, staring at my little black overnight bag, thinking how strange this was. I was thinking, *what is this doing here and how did it get here? What in the world is going on here, Lord?* At first I did not even think to open it and look inside. I just stood there pondering this situation. Suddenly I felt a strange sense of wonder coming over me and curiosity got the better of me. I unzipped the night bag.

Oh my dear Lord. I almost fell to my knees in the snow. The smell of ether escaped from the bag and the odor slapped me right across the face. In that instant, I knew what God had been doing. I had just found my son's meth lab!!!! I began to shake all over. Instantly I cried out to God to help me, to give me the strength to handle this situation. I could not believe what I was looking at. There were crushed pills, the ether and all the equipment to make meth. I ran to the house with it and fell to my knees before the Throne of God.

If anyone had come to the front door that day, they would have thought there was a crazy woman inside the house. I guess in some ways there was. I was crazed with the determination that Satan would not win my son's soul nor was he going to win this battle with drugs. I destroyed each piece of this mess, rebuking Satan, binding and loosing addicting spirits, drug dealers and ungodly desires from my son in the name of Jesus. I knew this was my right and responsibility as a child of the King and as a parent. He promised it to me in Matthew 18:18. I began an immediate fast and stormed the altar of God. I spiritually threw my son at His feet and quoted all the scripture I could think of to protect and restore my son to the Lord. I reminded God that Matthew belonged to Him. From day one, he was His, and He had even given me a prophecy over him. I claimed it over and over again. I quoted the scripture of Matthew 18:18 over and over again: "Whatsoever is bound on earth is bound in Heaven." I bound drugs and alcohol from Matthew. I bound Satan and addiction from his life. I bound all the demons of drugs, alcohol, addiction, selfishness, anger, pain, perversion and anything else I could think of from Matthew and the grip of sin on his life. Then I claimed the second half of that scripture: "Whatsoever is loosed on earth is loosed in Heaven." So I loosed a band of Angels around my son to protect him, to deliver him from the desires of this world and keep all the evil influences away. I prayed that anyone he went to for drugs wouldn't be home, couldn't be found, or, if he did find somebody, that there just wouldn't be any drugs available. I prayed for all open doors to be closed and I even went through our home and destroyed anything left that I thought was inappropriate or unacceptable to the Lord. I got rid of questionable movies, music and everything related to my backslidden life. I literally cleaned house for God and surrendered all to Him.

To tell you the truth, I can't be exact about everything I was praying because I was so wrapped up in the Spirit and in His presence. I believe the Holy Spirit took over my prayer language and was leading my prayers, my thoughts and my words. He had purposely led me to the woodpile to find its contents. He would not leave me now to fight this battle alone. The Holy Spirit was there in that room, taking my prayers to the Throne of God. My Father knew this day was coming. He had known of this day the day Matthew was born; He even knew of it from the beginning of time. His Word tells me so. Ephesians 2:10 tells us, "For we are God's workmanship, created in Christ Jesus to do good works, which God prepared in advance for us to do." Also, Acts 15:18 says, "Known unto God are all his works from the beginning of the world." And now, here He was leading and guiding me through this whole situation. He knew what I needed to do as a mother and a prayer warrior. The Lord had been preparing me and teaching me, rapidly, for months, for this day. It was overwhelming, the urgency to go to the throne of God for my son. And I did. I did not hesitate. I spent that day and most of the night in His presence. The Lord gave me a Scripture that day to claim over my Matthew. It was Psalm 91:11. "For He shall give His angels charge over thee, to keep thee in all thy ways." I claimed it for Matthew and I loosed a band of angels around my son that no foe could penetrate. I completely trusted in God to move mightily and miraculously in this situation. He had just proven to me without a doubt His love and concern for our Matthew and I knew he belonged to Him.

Matthew did not come home that night.

The next morning I went and picked up his Grandpa Rod from my sister's house; he has recovered from alcoholism for over twenty years. We went by the house Matthew was staying at to give Gene a phone message. I had to see Matthew. I had to let him know the lengths the Lord had gone to for his safety and I had to let him know how much God loved him. I needed to tell him everything that had transpired the day before and I needed to see my son.

Both of the boys were still sleeping when we got there. Matthew was sleeping on the floor lying in front of the wood stove. I banged on the door until he opened it. Once he opened the door, he quickly lay back down and covered his face with his blanket. It was a freezing cold January morning and he was hung over.

I had been desperately praying that God would help me to handle this HIS way, that He would help me to not let my "self" get in the way of my own fears and my motherly instincts, that my own feelings of anger and disappointment would be overshadowed by Christ's love and that I would be able to handle this situation the way Jesus would. I kept hearing in my heart that "Jesus handled everyone with love." Over and over again this thought kept coming into my heart and my mind. I know it was the Holy Spirit keeping all this turmoil and emotion from getting out of control. It very well could have turned into an ugly confrontation. The enemy wants not only to destroy our lives, but our relationships as well. He wanted to destroy us as a family and my life as a witness to the love and mercy of Jesus Christ. One wrong angry word could have cost us everything. Everything the Holy Spirit had been working to bring about lay in the balance of choosing to listen to Him and follow His leading or listen to my flesh. I knew I had to completely depend on Christ and be obedient to His voice. The enemy was NOT getting any more strongholds on my family.

  I found Matthew's friend still sleeping in his room and there was no waking him up, so I gave Matthew the message for Gene and told him, "By the way, I found your meth lab in the wood pile."

He lay there quietly for a few moments. I gently kicked the bottom of his foot and asked him if he heard me. With his face still covered, he said, "Yeah." I stood there shaking from head to toe and I asked him what he had to say for himself. He asked me what I did with it and I told him I threw it all away. Complete stillness. He knew his Grandpa Rod was standing beside me. I could feel the frustration and anger welling up inside me so I quietly reached out to Jesus. Matthew jerked the covers down from his face, glanced at his grandpa, and then looked at me angrily and said, "I want you to know you just threw away four thousand dollars!" Without hesitation I asked him if that was all the price of his soul was worth. After a moment he said, "Not now, Mom. I can't handle this now," and he covered his face back up. My step-dad and I stood there a moment as I let the Holy Spirit check my heart and calm me. I know my step-dad was praying silently for Matthew. I told him I loved him, his Grandpa told him he loved him also, and we left. I was so distraught. I could not believe, after all he had accomplished and come through this past year or more, that he would throw it all away so easily. And before he was even out from under all the other trouble he was still facing. All I could do was continue in prayer for him and trust in

God to bring this around into something beautiful for Matthew's future.

I believed God's word for him in Isaiah 61:3. "To appoint unto them that mourn in Zion, to give them beauty for ashes, the oil of joy for mourning, the garment of praise for the spirit of heaviness; that they might be called trees of righteousness, the planting of the Lord that He might be glorified." I believed that this was still part of the "much sorrow and pain" Matthew was to endure before God's prophecy could be fulfilled in his life. I just knew God was going to turn these ashes into something beautiful. I had His promise on it.

My step-dad was such a help to me. I had stayed the night before at my sister's, and he and I had stayed up late talking and praying for Matthew. I was so desperate for God to renew Matthew's heart and mind. I expected God to help us become a complete family in Christ. I know God had my step-dad there at this time just for this reason. His reasons, timing and ways are so much higher than we can comprehend, and they serve more than one purpose. He is a good God.

7

A PROFESSION OF FAITH

On Thursday, my husband stayed home from work and took my dad, my step-dad (who are obviously friends), my niece, and me out for the day. Dennis is a journeyman plumber and he gets to design and help build many million dollar homes. He wanted to show us some of these mansions he had worked on, so we went to view some of these magnificent homes and he gave us personal tours through them. We spent the morning enjoying the life of the rich and then we all went to lunch at our favorite fish restaurant. It was a fun day of visiting and fellowship.

We dropped everyone off at each one's destination at the end of the day, and later that night we went back to my sister's house for dinner. I didn't expect to see Matthew until the next day, Friday, and then only maybe. He had an appointment with his lawyer that next day, and it was supposed to be his last one. Court was scheduled for that following Tuesday, the twenty-eighth of January.

We arrived home from my sister's house after dinner and nevertheless, there he and Gene were, watching television. Matthew and I just looked at each other and did not speak. He was lying on the couch and glanced at me as I came in the door. There were no bad looks, no angry looks, just a quick glance between mother and son. He had broken my heart so badly. I just went into my room, got ready for bed and kept praying. His dad was very glad to see his boys so he stayed up with them for awhile. After Dennis came to bed, Matthew and Gene stayed up late watching the History channel. There was a documentary on that was about Cain and Abel. When it was over, Gene went home and Matthew went upstairs to bed.

The next morning I got up and began my Bible studies. I was praying for God's wisdom and love to deal with this day. I loved my son so very much and I truly believed he had a calling on his life. God had promised me. Not only by His Word, but through that prophecy of so long ago. I was still believing.

My heart's desire was to be lead by the Holy Spirit and let Jesus reach my son's heart and spirit. I had put it all in God's hands.

I was doing my school work, writing an essay on "What salvation means to me," when Matthew came downstairs in his boxer shorts and stood next to the wood stove. He looked so handsome standing there, my little boy all grown up. He was now a man of twenty-three years and it was time for him to take a look at his life, an honest look. I was praying that now was the time and he would do this.

It was a cold January morning and the stove felt so good to snuggle up to on those kinds of days. I didn't look up from my work at first. He stood there looking at me for a few minutes and finally asked, "Are you still mad at me?"

I responded without looking up. "I'm not mad at you Matthew."

There was a moment of silence before he asked, "Well, are you ever going to talk to me again? I hate it when you won't talk to me."

As I closed my books, sat back in my chair and looked him in the eyes, I told him, "Yes, I'll talk to you, but I just don't know what to say."

Without any raised voices or harsh words, and with our undivided attention to one another, we began a conversation that would ring in my heart forever. It was a conversation about God. We talked about His will for our lives and what He expects from us as His children.

Again I reminded Matthew of the promise God had spoken over his life and I asked him what he was going to do about it. I expressed that he needed to start walking with Jesus. At that point, he turned to me straight on, put his hands on his hips and point blank asked me, "Don't you believe I have Jesus in my heart!?"

He took me by surprise by being so offended by my comment. I told him, "Well, yes."

I did believe he had Jesus in his heart, I knew it for a fact, but I also knew he was not living the life God had for him and he really needed to stop willfully sinning. At that point he told me he did not know why he did the things he did, he did not mean to, and most of the time did not want to. He really wanted to do the right thing, but it was hard. More than anything he hated being a disappointment to his dad and me. His heart was so open. As he talked, I realized he was speaking the words of the Apostle Paul in Romans 7: 19: "For the good that I would do, I do not; but the evil which I would not do, that I do." His heart was willing, but his flesh was weak. Matthew 26:41 tells us, "Watch and pray, that you enter not into temptation; the spirit indeed is willing, but the flesh is weak."

We must have talked for an hour. At one point he asked me how in the world I had found that meth lab and I told him of how the Holy Spirit had led me to it.

It was the only explanation. I told him how the Lord kept urging me to look in the big log pile. He could not believe it. He said it had been in there for awhile and he had actually forgotten about it. He said he had planned on moving it, but never got around to it. I know he did not completely understand the working of the Holy Spirit that led me to that bag, but I made sure he understood that God loved him so much that He called on me to find it and to intervene through prayer and fasting. It was a miracle God had performed just for him and I told him he better start listening, because God was definitely watching over him. There was no denying it. Matthew was amazed and I could see it in his face as he pondered these things in his heart.

He had to get dressed and we needed to get ready to go see his lawyer. As he headed back upstairs to get cleaned up, we said "I love you" to each other, and up he went. I thanked God for being in the middle of that conversation! His presence had surrounded us. He had filled me with His patience and wisdom and most of all, His love for my son. I loved my children more than life itself, but there is a supernatural love that comes from God alone. Agape love. And our house was engulfed in it that morning. As a mother, I could have handled this in the flesh, crazed with anger and fear instead of filled with a supernatural love and peace. I was so pleased with how all this had transpired. There was no mistaking the anointing of the Holy Spirit and His supernatural presence throughout the whole morning.

We continued to talk and enjoy our time together on the way to the lawyer's. Out of the blue, he asked me "Did you know Cain and Abel are the first murder recorded in history?" I said yes I did and asked him what had brought that on. He told me he and Gene had stayed up last night and watched a documentary on it. Then we talked more about God and His love and the way life works. We discussed Cain and Abel's sacrifices and how God wants our best. He gave us His best, Jesus. We should always offer Him our best! I saw evidence in his heart of a true love for Jesus and a desire to do the right thing. I felt I was seeing the beginning of a curiosity and a hunger for God's Word. My prayers and hopes were reaching to new levels. I just knew this was the beginning of a life devoted to Christ that I had prayed for all of Matthew's life. It was the beginning of the prophecy of eighteen years in waiting being fulfilled.

Once at the lawyer's, we sat in the lobby and Matthew teased me and we chatted and joked around while waiting for the lawyer to finish with another client. Our attorney came out a couple of times to apologize to us for taking so long. I knew the waiting was tough on

Matthew but he was being very patient. When we finally got inside the office, the moment was there. What was going to happen to Matthew?

We had spent the last year and a half not having a clue what was going to come out of this or how long he would get. He knew he was going to do time, but fifteen years was uncalled for and way out of proportion to his crime. This dark cloud that had been over his head for so long only took a moment to disappear. Charley, our attorney, had gotten them to agree to thirty days in county jail, five years loss of driver's license, and two years probation!!! Our prayers had been answered! God had intervened in Matthew's life once again. It was a day to celebrate. Charley visited with us awhile. He really liked Matthew and wanted to see things go well for him. A couple of times over the year and a half we knew Charley, he had asked us at different times how a nice kid like Matthew had gotten into so much trouble. He couldn't understand how a kid with such a good heart could be sitting there in his office. Charley was a real man-eater when it came to defending his clients, but Matthew had touched a soft spot in his heart. He told us several times he really liked this kid. He gave us three mugs and three cooler cups with his logo on them and told us to tell Dennis hello and that he would see us Tuesday in court. Matthew was so relieved. He had that bounce in his step that had started to fade again with the use of drugs. The weight had been lifted and he was my Matthew again.

We stopped by the bike shop to check on his motorcycle that had been in there for months. It was almost finished, but they needed three hundred and fifty dollars and it would be done. He immediately started in on me to borrow the money so he could ride his bike before he went to jail. I told him we'd have to ask his dad first. He was antsy about it, but agreed.

On the way home Matthew wanted me to take him to Gene's house. He had promised Gene he'd come over and tell him the news when we got done at the lawyer's office. I told him I had taken out steaks for us for dinner and I wanted us to have a family dinner together to celebrate. He wanted Gene to join us. They were inseparable. They were both "our boys," so we stopped at the meat market and I bought Matthew a special, fat juicy porterhouse steak for dinner, dropped him off at Gene's and went on home.

I told Dennis everything that had transpired that day and at the lawyer's office. We were both so relieved that all of this was almost over. We were seeing the light at the end of that legal tunnel. I told him that the boys would be coming home for dinner and it was going to be a good one. We grilled the steaks and made garlic mashed potatoes and salad. It was a fun family dinner. We were all elated. The atmosphere was filled with relief, peace and joy. I know most of their celebrating was over the outcome of the day, and much of mine was, too, but my peace and joy were coming from the Holy Spirit. The air was charged with the presence of an almighty God at work. All of this was for a purpose. I knew this with all of my heart.

After dinner Matthew asked his dad for the three hundred and fifty dollars to get his bike out of the shop. He said, "Mom said it was okay with her if it was okay with you." I cracked up. He had used that line on both of us since he could talk, and I had not said that. I teasingly scolded him for that and his dad said no. Matthew wanted to ride that motorcycle so bad. That's all he wanted to do before he went to jail for another thirty days. He was frustrated, but accepted the answer.

He and Gene got ready to go out for the evening and he said, "If I'm going to jail for a month, I'm going to play this weekend."

I asked him to reconsider this but to no avail, so I told them to be careful and of course, said to them, "Do not get into any trouble!" They left, and I continued to pray that God would keep him in His hands. I had ended my fast that night at dinner, but continued to plead the blood of Jesus over Matthew and his future.

They did not come home that night, which was not unusual. Gene had his own place a few miles away from us, and they stayed there most of the time. Dennis had to work the next day, Saturday the twenty-fifth, and I had an all day rally in South County with the Home Interior's branch. I got home around four thirty that Saturday afternoon.

I was driving down our dirt road late that afternoon, headed towards home, when Matthew and Gene came flying by in Gene's truck. Matthew's hand flew up in a quick hello wave out the passenger's side window and then they were gone. I remember thinking to scold them when they got home for driving way too fast down that loose gravel road.

Dennis got home shortly after I did and he wanted to do something. He was wound up from the day and did not want to stay home. I, on the other hand, was worn out from my day. I had a headache and I was emotionally and spiritually drained from the events of the week. He asked me where the boys were and I told him I had just passed them flying by headed towards Gene's house. Dennis left for awhile and later on when he came back, he still wanted to do something with the boys, but they had not returned home.

Dennis wanted to go to the Riverboat that evening, but I didn't. I hate to gamble and do not enjoy that atmosphere, so I suggested he take my dad instead. Dennis did not think my dad would want to go, but he took off to give it a try. It was only about forty-five minutes later when the boys came looking for dad. I laughed at the irony and told them what had just happened. He was looking for them also to do something with him.

Matthew said, "You mean he went to the boat without us!"

I told him his dad didn't know where they were and Dennis had come back twice to try to catch up with them so they had missed out. Matthew asked for the garage door opener so he could get something out of the garage. We have a large detached garage that sits up the hill a ways from our house. We had hidden the garage door openers from Matthew after finding the meth lab, not knowing what we were in for, if the old Matthew was back and our possessions were not safe. We just weren't sure. Drugs and addiction are a powerful force and you really need Godly wisdom to deal with it.

So I got up and gave the door opener to him. I lay back down on the couch and talked to Gene a couple of minutes while Matthew ran up to the garage. He returned with a partial twelve pack of beer under his arm. He laid the door opener on top of my dresser and the two of them stood at the front door for a few minutes, talking to me but ready to leave. I asked where he was going with that beer and he replied, "To the bar." There was a little local place down the road, where everyone knows everyone. The boys would go there once in a while to play pool. It was something to do in such a small town. I told him he could not take beer in a bar and he proudly told me the owner lets him do anything he wants in that bar. He was quite a charmer with the ladies and a woman owned the place. Matthew was very much loved by all of our friends and most anyone who knew him. He had been taught to respect his elders and he was wonderful at doing so. The elderly and kids just loved him.

He bounced over and kissed me on my left temple and said, "Love you, Mom." I said, "I love you too, and behave yourselves and DO NOT get into any trouble!" They were joking and laughing as they went out of the door and they promised me they would be all right. They were so happy and care free, not a moment's thought as to what tomorrow would bring. They were living for the day.

Dennis returned home from the boat about an hour later. He and my dad had had lots of fun, but he still wanted to see his boys. I told him where they were and he asked if I minded if he went to catch up with them.

He wanted to share the wealth and give them some of the money he had won that night. I told him to go. As I look back now, I still see God's hand at work, giving us these last precious moments with Matthew, even if they weren't in the most perfect of settings.

Dennis came back home about an hour later. He had caught up with the boys at the bar and had played some pool with them. Dennis had a drink with them, gave them some pocket money and he left them there, still playing pool. He came on back home and we went to bed a little after midnight.

8

THE KNOCK ON THE DOOR

The next morning. I still have a hard time grasping what happened. At seven thirty a.m. we were awakened by a loud knock on the door. When I rose up out of my bed, I could see out the little panel window of our front door. There to my horror stood two police officers. One was a State Trooper and the other one was a Lincoln County Sheriff. It is completely indescribable. That wave of pain that starts at your head and flows through your entire body. That wave of fear and panic. You know it's serious, but you deny it. You do not want to accept it. I knew immediately that Matthew was dead. I fell back against the headboard and cried out to God." NO!" Dennis was asking me who it was and then he saw my panic stricken face. Just as suddenly, I thought, "No, it's not that bad. No, it's not Matthew."

"Who is it?" Dennis asked me again as I jumped out of bed. "It's the cops. I'm going to choke that kid if he's gotten into any trouble." Denial. It took every ounce of my strength to convince myself this was not real. It was just a small problem. God would not take my son away. Not now. Not before God's prophecy had been established in his life. I think Dennis rolled over and froze. Everything was becoming hazy and dreamlike and I lost track of my husband. As I got partially dressed, I wondered out loud what the boys had done now. My head was reeling. I know in my heart I knew. There was just no way I could believe God would do this to Matthew. I had a promise over Matthew's life and his death was not included in it. Not this early. He was only twenty-three years old. I just kept denying what I already knew in my heart.

I opened the door and asked what they wanted, what was wrong? I was filled with so much anger at them for being there. The State Trooper asked if they could come in. At this point my head was reeling out of control, my heart was pounding and I could barely stand. I could tell by the look on the officer's face this was serious and he did not want to be there. *Please God, don't let this be happening!*

As I stepped aside to let them in, the officer said there had been an accident. I asked the officer how bad it was and he lowered his head and shook it from side to side. Fatal.

Dennis was now lying across the bed where he could see us and I began to hear moans of grief coming from our bedroom. I asked these men if they knew what had happened. They told me there was a single vehicle accident, that there was alcohol involved and my son did not survive. "No, it's not my son. My son does not drive." I yelled at Dennis to stop crying because it was not Matthew, it was Gene. Gene's poor mother had now lost her second son. We had to go be with the family. It seemed like no one else was moving but I was spinning frantically in circles. Everything around me was deathly still, but I was whirling, spinning, denying, begging God, but still not wanting to believe this was happening. I asked about the other boy. It was his truck. It had to be him. Where was he? The officer said no one else was there. They had walked the accident scene and the field and found no one, just my Matthew. He had a hard time looking at me. In fact, he spent most of our conversation looking at my kitchen floor. The county officer never said a word. He just stood behind the Trooper and stared at me.

I still said "NO, Matthew did not drive." He did not have a driver's license and Gene did all the driving. He had just gotten out of so much trouble and he wouldn't take that chance. It just could not be him.

Dennis got up to get dressed. The officer asked me if my son was bald, if he had shaved his head. I vaguely remember groaning, "NO, NO, NO, it's *not* him. Oh God, please do not do this. NO, it's not him. We have to go. It's Gene. Not my Matthew." In all this confusion, Dennis had come out of the bedroom and was trying to make some sense of this with the police.

I could feel anger rising up inside of me toward Dennis because he seemed to be accepting what was happening. He wasn't putting up a fight. Then there was no denying it. The officers described my son to a T. My Matthew was gone. God had let him die, crushed by a truck, all alone, and in the cold. We had to go. I had to see for myself, I had to see my son. So many questions that needed answers began to flood our minds. All I knew was I had to get to the hospital and see if it really was Matthew. God wouldn't do this to me, especially as close as we had been lately. Everything He had been doing in our lives had pointed to such a different future. It DID NOT include Matthew dying, not now, not before us, not when everything was at its best for him in years.

I shut the bedroom door to finish getting dressed and told Dennis it was not Matthew. He seemed to know it was. He just cried and moved slowly. We stepped out of the bedroom and the officers were still standing there. I remember walking up to the State Trooper and hugging him. I really do not know why. He had such a compassionate look on his face and at that point I think we both needed consoling.

Dennis asked them more questions, but I did not hear. I did not want to hear. It was not my Matthew. "Gene's poor mother!" I could not believe she had lost a second son. *What would Matthew do without Gene? He's going to take it hard. We have to get to him.* I kept telling myself these things over and over.

As we started out of our front door to go to the hospital, Dennis noticed Matthew's quilted flannel jacket hanging on the coat tree by the front door. He stopped and picked it up and turned to me. He wrapped Matthew's jacket around my shoulders and squeezed it tight in front of me. We stood there for only a very short moment, but that was all we needed. Our eyes were locked together and without a word we began to try and prepare ourselves for what was facing us.

Matthew had left a pack of cigarettes and a lighter in the pocket. I clung to that jacket for days. I could not let go of it. It was a piece of him that still had his scent on it. This was so very important during this time. We held on tightly to these things so it would not seem as though he was completely ripped away from us so suddenly. We needed to feel him, we needed to smell him and we needed to cling on to anything and everything we could of his.

Then we stepped out of our front door. The officers had stayed outside in their car and watched us get in our truck and leave. That's when they pulled out behind us and left. They had radioed ahead to the hospital to let them know we were coming. I knew in my heart that this had been a difficult day for that Trooper.

Dennis went to Mansion Road first. He had to see for himself. This is where the Trooper told us the accident had happened. We found the accident site and there were pieces of Gene's truck strewn all down the road. He got out and was walking the area. I did not get out, but we could tell almost step by step what had happened. I began to lose control. I was losing my grip on denial and hate for my Father began to well up inside of me. I couldn't take it there. It made it too real. We had to get to the hospital. It was not Matthew. I would show them. Get me off that road and get me to the hospital!

We entered the hospital doors and I told a receptionist that someone had told me my son was there. She sent us down a hallway that seemed to grow longer with every step we took. I remember the anger in my voice at the inconvenience for being called there for no reason. It was not going to be my son. The next receptionist at the emergency room waiting area asked us our names. When we told her, she got up immediately and went into the emergency room. We heard her tell someone, "The Knoxes are here." Then she took us into the emergency room and led us to a closed door. A man was standing by it and he introduced himself as the coroner. He apologized to us for our loss, which infuriated me. I was prepared to look upon someone else's face when he opened that door. He stood with his hand on the doorknob as my Dennis and I stood at each other's side and braced ourselves. He slowly opened the door and to our horror, there he was. The top of his head was facing us as he laid lengthwise down the small room. I heard Dennis begin wailing behind me as I ran to my son. He was wrapped in bedding, and his beautiful face was uncovered and perfect. I quickly looked away and cried, "Oh my God, what have You done! It is my Matthew. My only son, lying on a gurney, dead!" Dennis stayed outside the doorway. I fell across my Matthew's body. The words, "Take up your bed and walk," ran through my head, but I could not speak them. It was a fleeting thought that quickly disappeared into the other sounds that began to take over the room. These strange moaning, groaning, travailing sounds were all that I could manage to come out of my mouth, but inside I screamed at God for His cruelty. There is no explaining what I heard in my head and my heart next, except the voice of the Holy Spirit. These were not the thoughts of a grief stricken mother but all of a sudden I heard the words, "Peace, look at the peace." They came to me over and over. These sweet, soft words could not be drowned out by the sounds of pain. But I did not want to hear from God at this point. I hated Him so much. None of this made any sense.

I could not bring myself to look at his face again for what seemed like forever. If I didn't look it wouldn't be true. I heard Dennis scream at someone to stop touching him. I heard his grief, but there was nothing I could do to help him. This was the trial of our lives and it was one that we had to face together, and in many ways, alone. I still kept hearing the words, "Look at the peace." Even in my pain I knew those words were not mine. I could not even fathom the thought of peace at a time like this. But I obeyed. I finally raised my head up from his chest and I looked at my boy's face. It was so sweet. He was beautiful. There was that handsome face we so dearly loved. It was true, this was my Matthew and he was gone from this world forever. There was just a trickle of blood from his nose, and a little from his ears. His eyes were shut and his mouth was spaced open just enough to see the bottom of his front teeth. He looked like he was sleeping. He looked like he was in a perfect, restful sleep. His cheeks glowed. I kissed his sweet face. He was still so soft and yet so cold. It was my Matthew. This was our son, my son, my only son, and my baby boy. He had been ripped from our arms way too early in life.

This was still my son. I knew that I knew that I *knew* that he was still there. I know his life was gone and he was not breathing. It had been hours since his accident, but there was a presence in that room that assured me Matthew was still there. I do not understand it nor can I explain it. I just know. God had granted me the opportunity to say goodbye.

We did not understand. What had happened? Why was he dead, why was he alone, and where was Gene? This just didn't make any sense. God would have warned me. Satan took my boy. How could this be? My mind was crazed with thoughts of anger towards God yet at the same time I would bounce back to crying out to Him for help and answers.

They took us to another room and asked us to wait a few moments. They needed some information. I do not really remember much of what happened then. I just remember us sitting there alone in a small break room not knowing what to do next.

After a while someone came and got us and led us back through the emergency room. The Coroner was still standing by the door so we stopped by one more time to say goodbye. I had to give him one last kiss.

The Coroner handed me his personal possessions—his wallet and his key ring with the initials M. K. One last look, one last hug, and one last goodbye. That was still my Matthew. The next time I was to see him, it would only be his shell. He was gone from me. What had God done? Had He made a mistake? Whose hands were on my son's life in his last moments? Had I mistakenly trusted in a God who loved us so little? A God who could cause us so much pain? And most important of all, where did Matthew go? Was he in heaven or hell? I decided at that moment that I would not continue to serve a God who would send my son to hell. He was a good boy even with all his troubles and heartaches. He had confessed Jesus was in his heart, but I just didn't know. I could feel this fear welling up within me that is was possible Matthew had gone to hell for eternity. This was quickly becoming more than I could bear.

We finally left the hospital and Dennis felt he had to go right straight back to the crash scene, so we went back to Mansion Road. After so long a time of trying to figure out what happened, he headed towards Gene's house. He was desperate to find out where Gene was and why Matthew was alone. I pleaded for him to take me home. I had phone calls to make. So many people needed to know and so many hearts to be broken, and I had to do it. He got me to the house and helped me inside. My body was weak and limp and was shaking almost uncontrollably. My first call was to Stacy; she was the closest and could get there the quickest to help me. Dennis just drove off.

I dropped to the floor with the phone in my hand at the entrance to the kitchen. That's as far as I could make it. I managed to call Stacy. She could not understand what I was saying; all she knew was that something had happened to Matthew. Apparently I was screaming that Matthew was in hell and she was thinking I said in jail. She was wondering why I should be so upset about that; it certainly wasn't the first time Matthew had been in jail. She thought he must have really gotten into trouble this time for me to be so upset. I believe that was God's way of protecting her till she made the drive over to me. Once she got to me, she would understand.

I called the pastor next. He was the next closest and had had a burden in his heart for Matthew and Gene. He was stunned and confused. You could hear the turmoil in his voice. I do not remember what was said other than they were on their way.

Sabra, my daughter. Oh dear God, how was I supposed to tell my girl her only brother was dead? This was so unfair. They had worked so hard on rebuilding their relationship. They were growing into adulthood together and now it was over. Just like that, in the blink of an eye. The finality of it all was too much to absorb.

I called the house she was staying at and they got her on the phone. Just hearing her voice sent such a pain through me I almost passed out. I had to keep it together. I had to get the words out. I was so concerned for her getting upset and driving. I remember reaching out to God for help, thinking to Him to please let her get to me safely, then jumping right back to the anger at Him for even letting this happen to begin with. This was all God's fault. He could have prevented it. After all, He is GOD. He created us, we pray for His protection. Where was that protection for my Matthew? I had finally, more than a year ago come to the place where I could leave Matthew in His hands. I prayed the prayer! "Whatever it takes, Lord, I trust in You!" This is what I get for that prayer? He should never have let this happen.

Sabra could not understand what I was saying. My words did not make sense to her either and she told her boyfriend something had happened to Matthew and she had to get to me. We hung up the phone and I knew she was on her way home. Home would never be the same again.

Next, I had to call my dad. Here he was living alone and would have to make the drive by himself. Plus Matthew and Sabra were his only grandchildren. It was up to me to tell him his only grandson was gone. This was so hard. All these calls were to tell all our loved ones that our Matthew was dead. There was so much grief, pain and anguish in all their voices. I could tell they were not all understanding the full extent of what I was saying, but they did know something was terribly wrong.

Next, I had to call my Mom and my older sister in California. My mother, the minister, a representative of God. Mom had only been out there on vacation for a week. When she answered the phone and I heard her voice, I began to scream at her and she could not understand what I was saying either. Oh how I needed to spew my anger out to her. All I could get out was, "My son is in Hell!!!" She said I kept screaming it over and over. I do not remember much of it but I know my older sister took the phone from our mom and she knew instantly what was happening.

Stacy came in the door. She fell to the floor in front of me and tried to make sense of what was happening. She kept telling me everything would be okay. I could not understand her calmness. She grabbed me by my arms and looked at me in the eyes and said, "Now tell me what has happened. Where is Matt?"

I leaned into her face and screamed at the top of my lungs, "HE'S DEAD!!!"

I will never forget that look on her face as long as I live, the sheer terror and shock and pain all combined into one agonizing twist of her face as she began to scream to God too. All this while my mother and sister were still on the phone. I had just dropped it in my lap when Stacy came in and do not even remember hanging it up.

I was overcome with sheer terror at this point. The terror that gripped my heart came with the realization that Matthew was truly gone and that he had possibly gone to hell. There was no turning back for Matthew now. There would be no more second chances. This was final. Matthew was now in eternity.

I had felt sadness before at the loss of someone I knew, someone who had possibly gone to hell, but this was different. This was my son. My loved one. This great fear of him residing in hell for eternity left my insides shattered. I screamed to God for mercy on Matthew's soul.

The depth to which this pain reaches is unexplainable. There are no words that can aptly define how deep it goes and the extent of the hole that begins in your soul.

With each new phone call, I tried to avoid the word DEAD. I kept telling everyone he was gone. Then the pastor and his wife came in. Stacy took over the phone calls and so much becomes a blur after that. It was Sunday, order day for my Home Interiors business, so lots of ladies were calling to put in orders. Stacy took the calls and began to tell them what had happened.

I don't remember when Dennis finally came home. I know he could not find Gene. Matthew had died driving Gene's truck and Gene was the last one to see him alive, as far as we knew. We had so many questions for Gene. Where was he?

Sabra. I needed my daughter there. I barely remember her arriving. When I saw her face and the confusion and pain, it was more than I could bear. My mind went blank. I was sitting on our steps that led to my children's rooms. She walked up to me and told me everything would be okay. Angrily I replied, "No it won't! It will never be okay again. My son is dead!"

With one quick blow of angry words, I crushed her. In her grief, all she knew to do was to try and help ease our pain and I lashed out at her in anger. I had to feel this pain. In my heart I knew God had brought us to this and for some reason we had to go through it. I was determined to feel everything I felt He was laying on me. If my Father could dish it out I could take it. I was so angry.

I did not in any way mean to do this. I do not even really remember saying this to her. She was now my only child and I had just added to her pain. She wrote me a letter expressing her pain and I realized then how much I had hurt her. But once again, thanks to the grace of God and His intervention, she and I were eventually able to talk about this and to work it out. I had to ask her for her forgiveness and she graciously accepted, then we were able to grieve together. Not alone, each of us dealing with our own personal pain, but she and I had crossed a barrier and we were now able to connect on a new level. God is good.

Finally, Gene had arrived. Someone yelled out, "Gene's here!" and we ran out the door. As I charged toward him, I could see the agony in his face. He could barely walk or talk. Almost six months to that day he had lost his brother and now God had taken Matthew from him. He too was devastated and he did not seem to want to face us. He had given Matthew permission to drive his truck. I believe he felt guilty, but this had been a choice Matthew had made. No one was to blame.

I saw he was carrying Matthew's winter coat in his hand. I had just bought it for him for Christmas, the

Christmas that had just past a month ago. I lunged at Gene and grabbed it from his hands and covered myself with it. This was another piece of my son and I needed it.

Eventually Gene began to tell us all he knew of those last moments. Matthew had asked him if he could borrow his truck. Matthew had been gone quite awhile and when he didn't return with it, Gene became worried. All he could do was sit and wait. He had no other vehicle so he couldn't go anywhere, and he didn't have a phone so he couldn't call anyone.

Then the police arrived and told him what had happened. He ran to a nearby pay phone and tried to call us but we had already gone to the hospital, so he called the only other person he could remember a phone number to. His mother. She lived an hour away but she left immediately to come and get him. For some reason, instead of bringing him to us, she took him back to her house. But she finally got him to us so we could fill in the blank spots and ask our questions.

Different ones were leading us through the steps of getting through that first day. I remember, at one point, when all of the family was finally there with all of our closest of friends, that Dennis and I were lying on the bed crying and grieving. We were holding each other, so lost in this pain. It seemed like everyone that was in the house was around the bed. Someone was on the bed lying across us, and everyone was praying. I did not hear anything specific, but it was as if I could feel the prayers going up to heaven right to the throne of God.

At that point I felt it was too late for them; Matthew was gone. Prayers were too late for him now. But later on I understood those prayers were for us, our family, our friends and everyone that had lost Matthew. They were for us to get through this with a faith in an Almighty King who sits on the throne and who knew and understood all that was happening. But all I felt was anger and disappointment in my Lord. How could He hurt us like this? I said it many times: I would NEVER hurt my children like this, why would He do this? It was a bad decision, wrong choice, and only bad could come of it. What kind of God did I serve?

God had let my son die alone. Not only alone, but he was also in the cold. For a mother this was so horrible to imagine. Gene told us that Matthew had been drinking most of the night but had quit a few hours before he drove. They had left the bar together with some girl, then later on early that morning, Matthew decided to go try to score some meth just one last time before he went to jail. He had not found any or anyone at home to sell him some. I know that was due to all the prayers I had sent up to the throne of God to block all those opportunities from his path and break them from his life. The Lord had answered my prayer. Matthew had left someone's driveway way too fast, missed a curve, and hit a fence post. The truck went into a spin and then into a flip. Matthew had been thrown from the cab and the truck landed on top of him from his waist down. The coroner had told us that Matthew had died instantly, that he did not suffer. For some reason that was supposed to give us some sense of peace, but I did not find it very consoling. It was unnatural for a parent to bury a child. It was not the order of things. I wanted my son back.

For me all I could think was that he didn't have a chance to cry out to God. Why didn't God give him that moment? Was there enough time for that? The bottom line for all of these questions was, WAS MATTHEW READY TO GO? If God loved him so much, why didn't he wait till the prophecy was fulfilled and there would be no doubt as to where Matthew went?

9

THE MIRACLES BEGIN

Someone driving to work early that Sunday morning had come across an overturned truck on Mansion Road. He stopped to see what was going on and if any one was inside. As he came around the truck there laid my Matthew. This man fell on his knees beside Matthew to give him CPR, but quickly realized it was too late, so he called the authorities and waited for help to arrive. He had left his name with every official that showed up that tragic morning. He wanted this young man's family to be able to contact him if needed. I was desperate to know who had found my son. Who was this mysterious person that was out so early on a Sunday morning? Were there any last words, and was there anything he could tell me to explain this senseless accident? I had to find out who this person was.

Gene told us all he knew and I was so angry with him for not being with Matthew. No one was there to hold him in his fear, in his last moments before stepping into the unknown, no one to comfort and say they loved him and that he will always be in our hearts. He was just gone.

But at the same time I was extremely thankful that no one else had been hurt. I had begun to see little things that had happened that made a difference. No other cars were involved. No other person was hurt. And most of all, I was so very thankful that my son's face was so beautiful. There were no obvious injuries. God gave us that opportunity to gaze upon his face and see that precious peace. It did take a while for all of this to sink in. But my Lord is patient.

We stumbled through the next day, making preparations, picking out final clothing, a permanent burial place and all these final decisions for a loved one who has no choice in the matter. You make these decisions, hoping and praying it is what your loved one would want. As we made it through Monday, some of the crowd began to leave our house and stay at different places. We were left alone with our anger and our grief.

The next day I would have to look upon my son in that artificial state of burial. I could not sleep. I went into his room and began to touch, smell, and feel every object in there, all of his clothes, which were few. He had just cleaned out his closet for the new clothes he got for Christmas. No real possessions, a new stereo he had gotten for Christmas and two new shotguns. I was going through old letters from girlfriends and paper work from his job. All of a sudden I became aware of how little I had of him—just a few clothes, a stereo, a homemade tattoo gun, some pictures and his dog. Old Rusty Dog, who had been Matthew's tenth birthday present. He was a full-blooded Siberian Husky, now thirteen years old. He had outlived his master.

There was nothing else. Most of all, there wasn't a grandchild. I sat in the middle of his bedroom floor and pounded my fist on it in anger toward God. I felt so empty. My heart was slowly disintegrating inside of me. I thought the pain would be a little more bearable if I could know, without a doubt, that he was with Jesus. The act of sin he was in that night terrified me.

Suddenly that gentle voice reached through to me, again. As I screamed at God for leaving me so little of him, I heard it. That soft, gentle voice of the Holy Spirit came to me once again to give me comfort. "You were only borrowing him anyway." I jolted upright and dissected that for a moment. If I was just borrowing him from God, that means God took him back! Inside I felt a level of peace, but the grief crept in again. I wanted to borrow him for so much longer! Twenty three years was just not enough. I wanted so much more for him and more time with him. We just were not done with him yet. Matthew wasn't ready to die either. God had cheated us all. "I'm still angry with You. I don't want to hear this."

But, at the same time what a comfort to know God was hearing me. He knew my anguish and He loved me enough, even in my anger toward Him, to reach out and comfort my heart. "I was only borrowing him anyway!" Those words became a ringing bell in my head. It was astounding. That meant Matthew belonged to God. No one could take his life, his soul, his spirit, his body, without the complete knowledge and permission of the Almighty Father Himself. What a comfort this was slowly becoming. I began to see little glimpses of answers to all my questions. God's hands were on the situation. Nothing had happened without His approval.

I eventually worked my way downstairs to my room, and only by the grace of God was I able to get a small amount of rest. I prayed, "God give us the strength to get through the rest of our lives without our Matthew." Our lives had been changed forever.

We went through the wake and the funeral in shock and intense pain. We were in and out of awareness, but conscious enough to know it was a huge funeral and a massive tribute to our son. Over five hundred people came to show their respects to Matthew and our family. The procession to the cemetery was almost four miles long. Here was a young man who had touched many lives. This wasn't a man who had walked the straight and narrow. He was a man of the world, playing, partying, full of life and love of this world, but he knew who Jesus was. Matthew knew there was no other way to heaven or to God except through Jesus Christ, God's own Son, and he had accepted that with all his heart.

Many people came to us and told us of different things Matthew had said or done to touch their lives. They expressed what a good heart he had. A good heart. I know God looks at our hearts, not our outsides or our works. God looks upon the heart of a man and I reminded Him of this each time someone would say to us what a good heart our son had. But a good heart will not gain you entrance into Heaven. It is the repentance of sin and acceptance of Jesus Christ as the Son of God and a willingness to follow Him. Matthew had done all these things. The goodness of his heart that others saw was the evidence that Jesus was truly there. "I am the way, the truth and the life; no man comes to the Father, but by Me." These are the words of Jesus in John 14:6. This was more hope and peace than anyone could have ever imagined.

One of Matthew's friends of many years came to me and fell into my arms at the visitation. As he wept for Matthew, he reminded me of the time when they had met in junior high. I remembered it clearly. Matthew had brought this boy home one day and even I was surprised at this unusual friendship. This boy was a strange one and just didn't fit the mold of most of the kids Matt hung out with. When I asked him about it, he just told me this guy didn't have any friends and all the kids teased him, so Matthew wanted to be his friend. Matt thought he was cool and did not care what anyone else thought. This young man told me then that Matthew had been the only friend he had ever had through those tough school years. What a testimony that Matthew had been so much to this young man in his greatest hour of need. A true friend.

I was overwhelmed with all of these stories and testimonies swirling around in my head and in my heart. I began to become confused. All of a sudden everyone was so positive that he was in heaven. It seems like we preach all our lives for people to wake up and walk with God, go the straight and narrow, separate ourselves from the world, do not sin, and now all of a sudden, once they are dead, everyone seems to be so sure they are with God. I know everyone does not go to heaven. Sin is sin and sin in our lives separates us from God

So what did all this mean? What could God reveal to me through all this? Does this mean once saved always saved? This was something I had been taught was a lie of Satan to keep us from drawing into God's presence. It was to keep us from seeking a closer walk with God. Once we got saved we could go about life as usual. I was taught it was a constant struggle to stay in right standing with God.

What was happening? Who took my son? Did God or Satan? Was he taken in sin so Satan won him or was he in God's hands, through admission of belief in Christ, through the leading of the Holy Spirit in the days before, through the prayers of his mother claiming angels encamped around him to protect and keep him? How does this work? In my heart I was counting on God for the answer.

The days following loomed with heartache and despair. Dennis began drowning his grief with alcohol and work. His anger and grief were so overwhelming, plus he had to go back into the work world and try to go on with some sort of normalcy. Home became the place to release his pain.

Many of our friends had lost a child and we did not realize just how many until this happened to us. Many of them warned us to not let this destroy our marriage. About half of those had ended their marriages in divorce due to the inability to cope. They began blaming each other, taking their pain out on each other and using anything but God to ease the pain. That was the old devil at work seeking to destroy, pure and simple.

Dennis seemed confident this wouldn't happen to us; I on the other hand was not so sure. Not only was I dealing with the loss of my boy, but I was losing my husband too. He had disappeared into his work and a beer can. It looked to me like he was drinking his pain away instead of leaning on Jesus. Talking to each other was getting very hard and almost non-existent. I thought I had lost him completely, but he, on the other hand, expressed to me that he was tired of being the strong one and that he felt he was okay.

I truly felt the Lord had done me in. This loss was much more than I could bear and now my marriage was in danger. There was no good thing coming of this and I more than anything needed to know where my son went. Whose hands did he leave this world in? "Help me Jesus, I just can not take anymore of this pain!"

I could not worship the Lord anymore. All I could do was fuss at Him and tell Him what a bad decision He had made. Most of all I could not believe He would do this to me. He had not warned me nor had He prepared me. I never dreamed He would allow such a tragedy in my life. After all, I had endured plenty of pain and loss along life's road. This was never even imagined, not losing a child.

A couple of different times in the next weeks the Lord would make a scripture stand out to me for me to hang on to. I believe the first one was Psalms 37: 23 &24: "The steps of a good man are ordered by the Lord: and He delights in his way. Though he falls, he shall not be utterly cast down; for the Lord upholds him with His hands." This verse did not say a righteous, holy or perfect man, but a good man. In my human thinking, my boy was none of these; righteous, holy or perfect. But he was a good man. I had just heard story after story of how good the people who knew him thought he was. I heard of how special so many people said he was to them. They told us stories of how respectful he was to his elders and what a good heart he had. This was a verse to hold onto that was more fitting of our situation, but I also knew goodness is not the key to eternal salvation. Only Jesus Christ is and I knew Matthew knew Him. The verse also says that if he falls he will not be utterly cast down that the Lord holds him up in His hands. Matthew had definitely fallen down that night.

Matthew had been drinking too much the night of his accident and he was out looking to score some drugs. He had brought home a girl he did not know. In the Christian world, those were all no-no's. He had died committing sin. I just could not understand how everyone else was so convinced he was in heaven. How did that work? I was on a mission to understand and hear from my Lord.

After a few weeks of this eating away at me, and very little peace, I begged God to intervene. My marriage was weakening, my feelings for my husband, God, this world, everything, was clouded over with anger. I was all consumed with grief and pain at the loss of my son and possibly even his soul. I sat in my bay window looking outside, screaming at God to do something. I just could not take the pain anymore. I just wanted to die. The phone rang. First, it was my step-dad, Rod. He just wanted to call and see how we were doing and let me know Dennis was on his heart and he was making it his "mission" to pray us through this. I cried and confided in him awhile. We hung up and almost immediately the phone rang again. This time it was my pastor; he wanted me to know Dennis was on his heart and he was going to make it his "mission" to pray us through this and be there for him. I needed to hear this. I had no strength to hold my husband up in prayer. How could I? I could barely get out of bed and function myself. How could I be of any help to my husband or to anyone? I did not even trust God at this point. He had let me down when I trusted him with Matthew. How could I pray for His help for my husband and my marriage now?

But God knew what needed to be done. Christian men were taking on the task of praying for my husband because I just could not. I was not able to pray for any one at this time. This was between God and me and I was determined not to worship Him or pray to Him till He gave me the answers I was looking for. But once again I was witnessing God's divine intervention. He was sending people to pray for us, to stand in the gap and pray for Him to meet our needs. When we could not pray, He called on saints to do it for us; when we did not feel love for Him, He sent His saints to express it to us; when we were in such agony, He called on others to hold us up and pray.

The next day I had to take my sister to a physical therapy session for her knee. I was crying to her about my pain for Matthew and how I needed answers. She tried to assure me, but nothing she or anyone else said made a difference. I expected God to tell me. He had promised me He would. Matthew 7:7&8 says, "Ask, and it shall be given you: seek and you shall find: knock, and it shall be opened to you; For every one that asks shall receive, and he that seeks shall find: and to him that knocks it shall be opened." He said it. I believed it and it was time for me to hear Him.

After I dropped my sister off at her appointment, I again was fussing with my Lord and crying out about

Matthew's salvation. I was sitting alone in my car in a parking lot, mulling over all the encouragement and words of hope people had been speaking to me. All of a sudden words my older sister had said to me flashed in my head along with a picture. She had been trying to talk to me one day on the phone about the blood of Jesus. Suddenly those words hit me with a great reality: covered by His blood! Is that it? Is that how it works? Matthew confessed Christ was in his heart, he admitted he did things he knew was wrong and did not know why, but he meant to do good with all his heart. So was the Holy Spirit telling me those sins were covered by the blood of Jesus? That precious blood He shed so we could all be saved from our sins? I could see Matthew as he was called home that night. That God was not seeing Matthew in his sin, but He was seeing him clothed in crimson red. This was a spark of a new hope that had hit my heart. It was a new confidence and a new trust. It was slowly seeping through the pain. Little by little God's words kept chipping away through the grief into my heart. *"Look at the peace." "You were just borrowing him anyway."* I was finally beginning to see my answers more clearly. Matthew belonged to Jesus. He had confessed it just hours before. Yes, we still commit sins; no, we are not perfect. But that is our goal in life, to earnestly strive for perfection in Christ. But because we are in the flesh we will never reach complete perfection until we are made perfect, by Him, in Glory. God's commandment to us is to be like Jesus. We are to continually strive to be like Him and this is how we draw closer to God and learn to walk more in His Spirit and not in the flesh. This is the example Christ has set for us, but until we reach that time, we will still stumble and fall, and yes, we will even sin. But thank God for the blood of Jesus that cleanses us from all our sins, sins of a past, present and future. He died once and for all.

My Lord had given me a mental picture, a vision if you will, of this situation. In one of my Biblical Studies from college, the question was asked, "How do you see your sins?" I closed my eyes and immediately saw the hand of Jesus. It was rough, callused, palm up and opened wide. The word SIN was carved across the middle of His palm. Then a massive puncture wound began to appear in the middle of that word, as if the nail had just been driven in. Suddenly His blood began to ooze from that open wound and it covered the sin that was scarred deep in His hand. It became completely covered by His blood. Jesus was touching my heart with the reality of His cleansing blood. That was the crimson red I saw covering Matthew. It was the crimson red God saw covering Matthew. He was clothed in the blood of Jesus.

But Oh, the pain and agony of this loss that still filled the heart and soul of a grieving mother!

10

DID YOU KNOW MATT?

At this point in time I hadn't become a member of Church on The Rock just yet. My friends and I had still been having church in our homes and we called it Cross Roads of Life. It didn't take long after losing Matthew for all of us to begin to drift apart and eventually our little church broke up. I'm not exactly sure just what happened. Everyone was grieving so deeply that it was hard to praise, worship and celebrate. Some of Matthew's friends had come to our church and some had even asked Jesus into their hearts. Even in my anger I was still telling people they needed Jesus, because this could happen to any one of them at any time. So it was quite a blessing to know Matthew's life and death were being used for God.

It still hurt so much to know Matthew died alone and in the cold. How could God do this? I tried so hard to find out who found him. I had to see if he was still alive when they found him or if he had spoken any last words. But no one could help me. I called the Sergeant in charge of the accident that had come to the house that awful day. He remembered me and said he thought the coroner had taken a name and that my son was already gone when he was found. But that was all he knew. He asked how we were doing and told me he was very sorry for our loss. He had just come on duty that morning of the accident when he got the call to come to Mansion Road. He said it had been an agonizing drive to our house and he was sorry he had to do it. He wished us well.

I then called the coroner and he said he did not have a name, but he knew that I did not know the person. I asked him how he knew that if he didn't have a name and he said the man who found Matthew did not acknowledge he knew us. He said he would check with the other officers and EMT workers involved and he would call me if he found out anything. There was no one else to call and nowhere else to look. I put it in God's hands.

My heart was beginning to soften towards God. I had begun my school work again exactly one month to the day from when Matthew left us. I was dragging through the work slowly because it was so hard to concentrate. But I pushed on and as time went by and the more I was determined to settle this with my Lord, the more I could see and understand. The scriptures were starting to jump out at me. I was receiving the Rehma Word of God, not just the written. He soothed me with Psalm 34: 18&19, "The Lord is nigh unto them that are of a broken heart; and he saveth such as be of a contrite spirit. Many are the afflictions of the righteous; but the Lord delivereth him out of them all." He reassured me with 1 Peter 4:8, "Above all things have fervent charity (love) among yourselves; for charity (love) shall cover a multitude of sins," and He set my heart at peace with Galatians 3:26, "For ye are all children of God by faith in Christ Jesus." Matthew had expressed his faith in Christ Jesus less than twenty-four hours before his accident. What a relief Jesus was bringing into my inner soul.

A few days later I had to go to the cemetery to check on the flowers. It was early spring and we had had some bad weather with lots of wind and rain. I went out there two or three times a week to keep it nice. I got to his gravesite that afternoon and for the first time I actually sat for awhile. Most of the time I just checked everything out, cried a lot, wrestled with all of the emotions and went on home. This day, I stayed awhile; it was a nice day and I felt a little bit of peace there. I began to hear the Holy Spirit telling me to go to Mansion Road. I hated going there and I did not want that cross there to remind me of our loss. The guys Matt worked with at Willerding had made this beautiful six foot cross for us to put out on Mansion Road. I did not want it there. I had always hated seeing those crosses on the sides of the road and said if anything like this were to ever happen to any of us, I would not do that. I did not want to have to drive by one of those roadside crosses and be reminded of the death of a loved one. But Dennis wanted it and so did Sabra. Matthew's Aunt Stacy too, and it obviously meant a lot to his friends who went to all the trouble to make the cross for us. Dennis painted it and the day we put it up, there were twenty-two friends and family with us. We planted flowers around it and took pictures, and I promised myself I would never go back there again. I had hardly traveled that road before and surely would never again.

Stacy and Gene were supposed to be taking care of it, but it was very painful for them too, so I was not sure if anyone else was checking on it and keeping it up. After quite a bit of arguing with the Lord, I decided I should go. I fought this feeling for quite awhile. But it kept nagging at me and I knew I had to go and face this place eventually. It was only a few miles from the cemetery so it would not take but a few minutes to get there. I really dreaded it, but I knew I had to go.

I pulled up to this beautiful white and purple (purple was Matthew's favorite color) cross and parked with my emergency flashers on. In my heart I reached out to God for strength and help. I knew He had led me there for a reason and as hard as this was, I was praying it was a good one. This is where my son took his last breath. I wanted to find something of Matthew's there on that road. Something besides tangled truck mess. I wanted to find a note, a hat, anything personal of his that would turn this into a place of joy and peace instead of a place of hate and anguish.

Many of his friends and ours had been there and lots of things were hanging on the cross and around it. The cross was covered with flowers, cards, plaques, CD's, name badges and much more. It really was quite beautiful to see. I was surprised at the feeling of comfort I had at this place. It was so touching to know so many people loved him and were keeping him in their thoughts and hearts. They took the time out to come by and remember.

There were a few cars that would come by and slow down. A couple of times people stopped to see if I needed help or would start to pull over and I would wave them on without even looking. As I walked up and down the accident scene, I prayed God had me there to let me find something of his but I had no luck in finding anything. It had been a couple of months or more, and Dennis and I had walked this before. I found nothing. I had really believed in my heart I was there for a reason, but I could not find anything on the ground that was significant. As I prepared to leave, I walked up to the cross one last time to straighten some of the flowers and make sure they were secured tightly. I would not be returning for quite awhile. Never, if I could help it.

A large red SUV had pulled up and stopped on the road but I hadn't really noticed. They had pulled over and parked in front of my truck when I heard them, but before I could wave them on, the man driving leaned across his wife and asked me "Did you know Matt?"

I thought his words were quite peculiar because he seemed to know Matthew. He said this with some sort of familiarity. It sounded personal, like he knew my Matthew. I turned around to look at them and began to walk towards the truck as I said, "Yes, he's my son." Before I got to them, he looked at me with great intensity and relief on his face. His wife, I assumed, quickly turned to look at his reaction to my words, and as they both gazed back at me with tears in their eyes, he said, "I'm the man who found him!!!!"

"I'm the man who found him!" These words echoed through my head and I could not believe what I was

hearing. My knees buckled underneath me and I almost fell to the ground. I made it to his wife's door and she grabbed me and pulled me into her. We were all speechless. The three of us cried together for a moment, not speaking a word. We quietly were sharing grief and joy and the presence of an awesome God.

I was so overwhelmed by the love of God and how he could give me such a gift, especially after all my hatred, anger and fussing I had thrown at Him, but here it was. All His mercy, goodness, kindness, understanding and love all in one sentence: "I'm the man who found him." When words finally came out of my mouth, I expressed to this couple how I had prayed for that answer. It was one of my last questions to God that I needed answered. There around this man's neck hung a large gold cross. He was a Christian.

Questions began to flow. I asked him the most important one for me, was Matthew still alive when he found him? What could he tell me about what he saw there that morning and what had he felt? "No," he said, Matthew was already gone when he found him. He told me how he came upon this overturned truck on his way to work early that Sunday morning. He got out of his truck to check out the situation, never expecting to find what he did. All along he felt an urgency in his heart to let this boy's family know that he had stayed with Matthew the whole time up until the emergency people took him away in an ambulance. He had left his phone number with every emergency worker there, but no one had it for me. My heavenly Father did. My Father God kept this information from me. He had blinded these people from this information so He could give this to me Himself. This was His magnificent way of showing me He was present in every step of this journey. He knew every moment that had passed, He heard every prayer that was spoken and He felt every emotion that we had endured. He was involved in every part of this journey we had to live through. This moment was His gift to me.

This couple and I talked about the accident. We talked about the effect it had on him. He had been profoundly affected by that morning's events. He had gone on to work that morning discussing it with his co-workers. He was concerned about how we were doing and they had been praying for us. Eventually, I had to ask him a question that had been consuming me. That look of peace on my Matthew's face, did he see it? Was it there when he found him or did the hospital have something to do with it? Or was it even just my imagination? What did he see on my son's face?

He assured me with all his heart. He spoke to me the words I had longed to hear. He said, "Denise, if anyone had asked me at any time if I thought this boy was a Christian, I would have had to say yes. As I sat with him, praying over him and waiting for help, I felt that peace. This whole place was surrounded with peace. I had to stay with this boy and I knew I had to let his family know that the presence of God was here. I feel you can rest assured." He told me how he had felt an urgency to find Matthew's family and tell us this. He had been praying about it and once he saw the cross put up by the road, he continued to drive by it. He prayed that one day God would send him by when a friend or family member of Matthew's would be there so he could give us this message from God. God sent someone to be with Matthew and pray, and there was peace. He really was not alone.

11

ONE SET OF FOOTPRINTS

I was beginning to see what the Lord means when He tells us He's with us in those bad times, but we can't feel Him. This is the time to stop going on feelings and decide, do I believe? Am I going to trust Him in this and let Him do His work? Is this really the God I've trusted in all my life? Yes, He is. This is the good God who knew me before I was formed in the womb. This IS that loving, forgiving, all knowing and understanding Father I love. He is good.

This has happened for a reason and not just one. God works in many mysterious ways for many purposes. My Father was with me. My son had been dedicated to Him at birth, and he belonged to God. My God had truly shown He was with me through this, not in feelings, but in His Word and by His presence and through His physical biblical Word and His Rehma words to me. Even though I was at my angriest with Him, He had the time to talk to me. He listened to me and He was reaching out to me in many special ways. He was still answering my prayers and letting me know He is aware of this situation and my pain. I have the confidence and peace that my Matthew was in His hands and he never left them. Those hands carried him home. Those hands are the same hands that have carried me through this. Not just me, but my entire family that has trusted in Him to do so.

In August of that year, Dennis and I had woken up one Saturday morning and we were having coffee in bed. Our thoughts were still on Matthew, but trying to grasp on to some sort of normalcy. As we sat there in silence, God brought back to my memory of a time when Matthew was just three years old. We lived in California then and Sabra was about twelve months old. I had put them both down for their afternoon naps, and I was folding clothes in the living room on the couch. Out of the corner of my eye I saw the shadow of a figure dash around the corner of my kitchen and head down the hallway towards the kids' rooms. I sat in shock and in prayer for a moment, not believing what I thought I had seen. I eased off the couch and looked down the hall just in time to see this shadow disappear into my room, across the hall from Matthew's room. I really began to pray.

There was no mistaking a presence in the house. I fervently began to pray for the Lord's strength and protection. I never really felt fear, just a deep curiosity and wonder as to what or who this was. I began to ease down the hallway toward my bedroom and slowly peeked in around the doorway. This shadowy figure had disappeared again, this time into my bathroom. At this point I became angry at the thought of an intruder stepping on my turf threatening my children and me. I knew I had him cornered. One last quick prayer for strength and I burst into the bathroom. Nothing. I stood there for a moment in thought, wondering what was going on. I still felt no fear. I was completely baffled at what was happening but I knew without a doubt I had seen someone's shadow moving throughout my house. At that point I had no idea what had led me there or why.

Then I heard a noise in my shower. I gathered the sum of my strength, took a deep breath, said a quick prayer and shoved the shower curtain back. There to my surprise was my Matthew, sitting in the shower on the floor with his daddy's razor in hand, starting to shave his face. "Hi, Mommy!" my three year old exclaimed with a proud smile across his chubby little cheeks. "I'm shavin'!" I took the razor from him, picked him up and began to thank God for his safety. An overwhelming presence of God filled the house and it was then, at that moment, I realized the mysterious shadowy figure was an angel. An angel had drawn my attention to my son. My father had sent an angel to protect Matthew, to guard him and keep him safe.

I told Dennis of this memory and could not understand why *now*? Why had this memory been brought to my mind and why hadn't that angel protected him at his accident?

I prayed about this so much. I could not figure it out, but the memory played over and over in my mind. It was as clear as if it had just happened yesterday, but it had been twenty years ago. I could not shake it. I began to pray and ask God why He was doing this to me. What was the meaning of this memory coming back to me now, so intense and fresh, and what was the Lord trying to show me or tell me? It hurt to think Matthew had an angel as a baby, but not as a grown man.

Two weeks later, I went to my mom's house for the weekend. As we sat early on Sunday morning having coffee, I was crying to her and sharing my pain. I began to tell her of this memory. She had remembered something about it, but I went through the whole story with her again, step by step. When I got to the end of the story, where I realized an angel had led me to Matthew in my shower, there it was again. That soft, sweet, gentle voice I have come to know so well. That precious voice of The Holy Spirit spoke to me and said, "The same angel that was with him at three was with him at twenty-three."

Once again my heavenly Father was reaching out to me to meet my needs. God himself had refreshed that memory to me so He could give me another gift. This was one more assurance as to my son's fate. My answers were complete. Matthew is with Jesus.

He is the God of the Universe. He spoke it into existence and has every hair of our head counted.

I know in whose hands my son left this world. The hands of the angels the Lord had led me to pray for. Those angels that God had encamped around him to protect him. Those were the same angels that were with him since the day of his birth and since the day of his dedication to God. He belonged to God before he belonged to me. He was our gift. Temporary as it was, God had fulfilled His purpose in Matthew's life and called him home. I was more than assured of this. God Himself tells me so.

As I sat one day pondering on these things in my heart, I realized that Matthew was born on a Sunday, dedicated to God on a Sunday, prophesied over on a Sunday, saved on Sunday, baptized on Sunday, and taken home on a Sunday. The Lord's day. He wasn't a perfect young man, he was not even close. None of us are. But he had the heart of a true man of valor. He honored and adored his parents and family. He loved God and lived his life to the best of his "light." He was twenty-three years old in an evil, hardened world, and I know God loved him. He knew Matthew. He knew what was ahead of him and He loved him enough to have me intervening in prayer for him. He loved Matthew so much he led me to the wood pile that day so I would start praying and fasting for him. My Lord knew my son's name and his future. I had handed that little life back to Him a long time ago and I told Him I trusted Him with it. I still do.

We will always miss our Matthew with all our hearts. But each day that I wake up and I am still here, I know it is because God has not finished with me yet. My days are numbered too, and when they are up, I will see my son again. Oh what a day of rejoicing that will be.

As I look back at God's great mercy through this, I can see I have truly experienced the "Footprints" of God. As we stumbled through this heartbreaking time, I know God Almighty was carrying me through it. I can honestly say I have never felt His presence closer. I felt His Holy Spirit wrapped around me, comforting me, waiting for me to listen, and offering words of peace and comfort for my soul.

12

A CALL TO PARENTS

There are many promises of hope in the Bible for us and our children. The Lord has also shown me the spiritual authority and power we have, in His name, over them. Our children are a gift from Him. We have a great responsibility in the way we receive and care for these gifts.

It is of the utmost importance to dedicate our children to God. As soon as they are born it is our responsibility to offer them right back to Him. After all, they are His anyway. It is like tithing. Our first fruits belong to God, so just offer them right back to Him so he may accomplish His good and perfect will in their lives. His word promises us in Leviticus 27:28b that, "every devoted thing is most holy unto the Lord." God takes these acts of faith seriously and is faithful to fulfill all His promises to us. Then it is our responsibility to do our best to raise them in His ways. Bring them up in His Word, establish them in a church, encourage Godly choices in their lives, help them to choose Godly friends to associate with and most important of all, be a Godly example.

Children are born into this world every second. Some are born into Godly, caring homes and are given the best a parent can offer. Others are not so fortunate. Some are brought into the world in an ungodly, unloving and unwanted environment. This is not God's choice; it is man's free will choice. When we choose to go through life without Christ, without surrendering our will to the Father through His Son, Jesus, we leave ourselves open to the abuse and destruction of the devil and to spiritual death. The devil is our enemy. He seeks to destroy all God has created. The devil can only do this with our permission. When we refuse Christ, we refuse the heavenly Father's protection He has established for us. We alone allow Satan to have dominion in our lives. There is no in-between. In Matthew 6:24, God confirms, "No man can serve two masters; for either he will hate the one and love the other, or else he will hold to the one and despise the other. You cannot serve God and mammon." And also in Romans 6:23, "For the wages of sin is death; but the gift of God is eternal life through Christ Jesus our Lord."

Have you made that choice in your life today? Are you seeking help and wisdom in raising your children in today's world? Or are you seeking something for yourself? Is there something missing in your life? Do you feel empty and inadequate in all the things you try to accomplish in your life? Do you need help and wisdom and answers for your own life and the world just does not seem to have them? Your Heavenly Father does. You can only come into His presence through His Son Jesus Christ. There is only one way. Jesus said, "I am the way, the truth and the life. No man comes to the Father except through me." John 14:6.

I urge you to seek Him today. Ask Him for forgiveness for all your past mistakes and disobedience and surrender your life and your children's lives into His hands today. You too will see the miracles begin.

Matthew could never have given me a greater honor than to pray to God, "I just want what my mom's got." I fall to my knees in humble thanks for those words that he spoke to God and then shared with me. We do make a difference in our children's lives. Never doubt it for one second or take it lightly. We will stand before God and we will be held accountable for these gifts of life that He has blessed us with.

God is a good God. When we belong to Him, we can stand confident that He is working all things together for our good. Romans 8:28 says, "And we know that all things work together for good to them that love God, to them who are the called according to His purpose."

I do believe with all my heart that God did fulfill His prophecy over Matthew. I also know that it was not fulfilled in the way I had prayed for or that I had hoped for. Matthew had definitely known much pain and sorrow in his life. But through all of this he had kept a love in his heart for Jesus Christ. And when it came to the end, I truly believe he faced his last breath as a man of valor. Valor means "courage or bravery." In those last seconds of life I know my son saw his angels around him. I know that he knew he was facing eternity with his Lord and Savior and he accepted it with great courage. There is no other explanation for that glow of peace on his face.

Only another parent who has lost a child can truly understand this kind of pain and grief. I honestly believe there is no deeper wound or pain a person can feel than to lose a child, but Jesus is the healing salve to cover that wound.

We can hold on to them. We can hold on to their memories and we can hold on to their pictures. We also need to talk about them as often as we can. But be happy for them. Rejoice in the knowledge of their healing and their completeness in the presence of our Lord and Savior.

The holidays and special days that meant something to Matthew have been especially tough. But God has brought a peace that passes understanding and a special comfort for those days. As we passed our second Christmas without him, I realized, *What a place for Matthew to be on Christmas day, actually spending Jesus' birthday with Jesus Christ Himself.* There is no way I could wish him back into this world knowing that.

All of the holidays have been hard on us. And most of the time it does not take a holiday to hurt for that lost child. It is a pain that will never go away. Once we can come to a point in our lives where we rest assured that our child is with God, we then can realize it is only our own selfishness that keeps holding on to the pain.

I have reached a time now where I still, and will always, miss my son so much. But knowing exactly where he is, I would not wish him back here to this life. He is in the presence of our King, our Lord and Savior, God Almighty Himself. How could I want him back on earth?

I felt for a long time that our lives would never be the same. And I thank God that in many ways we are not the same, nor will we ever be again. But I am so blessed and so thankful to know that I can smile again. I can have a sense of humor again and I can enjoy the life the Lord has blessed me with, again. I can only do this through the strength and the presence of Jesus Christ in my life. He restores all these things unto us, when we let Him. Psalm 51:12 says, "Restore unto me the joy of thy salvation; and uphold me with thy free spirit."

I thank God with all my heart that I had a son named Matthew Dean for twenty-three years. He was a joy, a learning tool, and even a "thorn in my side" at times. I am sure any mother can relate to that. But above all, he was my gift and he belonged to God. I belong to God, my daughter and my husband both belong to God, and my heart is at peace with my heavenly Father. None of us have reached perfection. None of us are without imperfections and weaknesses. But ALL of us can be made righteous and washed clean by the blood of Jesus Christ. Matthew had been washed in that blood and was covered by it. I thank my loving and merciful Father with all my heart and my soul for assuring me of this. I leave everything else at rest in His hands.

Only a good God that loves us so intimately would prepare such a future for us. Our Father God and Creator is the ultimate parent.

His Word is our instruction book for all of life. All the answers to raising children, keeping a marriage and walking in the presence of God are all right there. God is good and God is love. Be good to your children and love them. We only have one shot at it. Make the best of it and do it God's way, by the Book. Consult it daily.

EPILOGUE

In April of two thousand and five I was flipping through our new satellite channels. I have never been one much for Tele-evangelists, except for my own Pastor Blunt of *Principles for Life*, of course, but I found myself in the religious channels sections. One program caught my eye. All it said was "Joni Lamb," but I was compelled to watch. It was the last ten minutes or so of the program and Mrs. Lamb was chatting with a gentleman seated on her couch. Before I could move on to the next channel, her guest said the words "Teen Challenge" and my heart was gripped. They spoke for a couple more minutes and as she concluded her show, she said to him, "Well, Alan, I want to thank you for being a guest on our show today. It has been wonderful hearing about all the great things God has done through Teen Challenge and your years working with the youth."

"Oh Lord, could this really be? Could this really be our Alan?" I copied the e-mail address on a piece of paper and planned on contacting them to see who this man was. But at this point it was so much nicer to believe this *was* my Alan from twenty years ago than it was to take the chance and find out it was not him. So I waited.

After about a week or so, I was getting ready to go to work and I decided to send a quick e-mail to the Joni Lamb show. I explained a little of my Matthew's story to the invisible face at the other end of the computer and I asked them if they could tell me who exactly this man was that was on the show that day and if they knew how I could contact him. I left with my hopes prepared to be crushed.

When I got home later that day, I ran to the computer to see if there was an answer from the show and to my surprise there was, but it was not from the show. It was actually from the show guest, Alan himself. He told me he had been the District Director of Teen Challenge over southern California back in the eighties, and it was possible he had spoken at my church. He asked me the name of my church and the name of the pastor, and what had happened to my son. I immediately sat down and I wrote him back. He was now an executive with Daystar Television and was currently living in Texas. I told him the name of the church but it had been so long ago I couldn't remember the pastor's name. I told him we had lost Matthew in an accident and how significant that prophecy had been in our lives. I sent the message off and waited anxiously for his reply.

It came back in just a matter of minutes. Yes, he had spoken at that particular church several times, he had traveled with the Teen Challenge Boys Choir, but it would be impossible to know if he was the exact Alan I was looking for since there were several Alans that worked with Teen Challenge back then. He asked me more about Matthew and he thanked me for writing.

In the mean time I had put a call into my mother who was back out visiting my sister in California. When my mom got on the phone I said, "You won't believe what's going on here!" I explained the details as I thoroughly enjoyed this possibility of God crossing my path with our Alan again after all these years. As I told Mom about this, she reminded me that she was the one who had met Alan in California when she was volunteering at Teen Challenge, and she had been the one to invite them to our church. She also told me that she and my grandmother had taken Alan and his wife out to dinner and found out that he was actually from the same town in Missouri that we were all from and my grandmother actually knew his grandmother. I was floored. At the same time my exuberance was crushed. There could be no stronger evidence to prove or not prove if this was our Alan than to know where he was originally from and confront him with this information.

So, with great hesitation I sent out my last e-mail to him. First I made my apologies for bothering him again and then I explained to him the story my mother had just told me. I told him if he was that Alan, this truly was a gift from God and a miracle. If he wasn't, then I thanked him with all my heart for his time and patience and for returning my e-mails and for listening. I told him it was a great honor to visit with him and I sent it off.

Within seconds he wrote back, "Yes, I am from Missouri!" Unbelievable! Those words opened a door from the past that suddenly tied right in to the present. We sent more e-mails and eventually we shared a wonderful conversation over the phone. Alan, in his obedience of speaking God's word to me during that phone conversation, had no idea he was giving me finality to many things I had been searching for. When I think of this gift, and I do that often, I still find it hard to believe that the Lord has crossed our paths again after all this time.

But I see this coming together as another gift from God to bring that precious prophecy around full circle. Matthew's life knew much pain and sorrow, I know he faced his death as a man of valor, with bravery and peace, and he was covered by the blood of Jesus. Now it is moving even further into the future through the testimony of this book.

You see, our Heavenly Father cares about every aspect of our lives. He cares about the very smallest to the very largest. He cares about the very smallest of our thoughts, our hurts, our hopes, our dreams, our desires, our prayers, our pains, our questions, our decisions and every movement of our lives. And if He cares this much for the smallest of things, just think of the love and mercy and care He has put into the biggest of things.

He offers that limitless love to us freely and wants to pour it into every part of our beings. It's up to us to step into it. When you pray for your loved ones, know that God hears you and is moving on their behalf and yours to bring about His best for them. When you trust in Him to do whatever it takes to get them into His Kingdom, He will honor your prayers. His ways may not be what we have in mind, but you can trust that He will do whatever it takes to save the lost.

The greatest gift God gave us was His only Son, Jesus Christ. That gift exemplifies that love. Jesus sits at our Father's right hand making intercession for us. In other words, He's telling His Father everything there is to know about us and pleading our case for us. His desire is to pour out all that love and mercy over all of us.

Won't you accept Him as your Lord and Savior today if you haven't already? Do you desire a direct line to The Father? You gain that through Jesus Christ and Him alone. You can't go wrong with Jesus. Just ask Him in and let Him work and move in your life today. That is when you can live a life trusting in His promises and filled with hope. That's when you will see the miracles begin.

In His Passing

In his passing he has risen,
From a man of doubt to a man of wisdom.

A man meant to be freed
From all the pain he suffered.
His voice and his laughter
Will always be heard.

The bells of his silence ring deep in our ears
But will always be seen through everyone's tears.

I'm touched by his words
I never before felt,
And captured by his scent
I never before smelt.

The power he held was great on this earth,
And substantial to all since the day of his birth.

By Sabra Knox
7/21/03

978-0-595-44716-9
0-595-44716-3

Printed in the United States
81670LV00003B/184-195